ARABIC COOKERY

ROSEMARY MACDONALD

foulsham

LONDON • NEW YORK • TORONTO • SYDNEY

foulsham

The Publishing House, Bennetts Close,
Cippenham, Berkshire, SL1 5AP, England.

Dedication

I dedicate this book to my son Niall, without whose wizardry on the computer this book would never have been finished. Also to Delmar, who ate the food, Sallie, the grammarian, and all my friends in Dubai.

ISBN 0-572-02145-3

Typeset in Great Britain by Typesetting Solutions, Slough, Berks.
Printed in Great Britain by St. Edmundsbury Press, Bury St. Edmunds, Suffolk.

CONTENTS

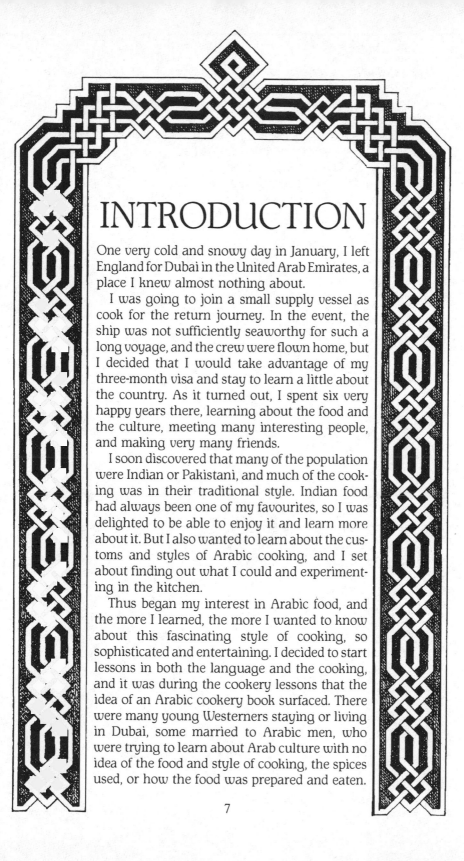

INTRODUCTION

One very cold and snowy day in January, I left England for Dubai in the United Arab Emirates, a place I knew almost nothing about.

I was going to join a small supply vessel as cook for the return journey. In the event, the ship was not sufficiently seaworthy for such a long voyage, and the crew were flown home, but I decided that I would take advantage of my three-month visa and stay to learn a little about the country. As it turned out, I spent six very happy years there, learning about the food and the culture, meeting many interesting people, and making very many friends.

I soon discovered that many of the population were Indian or Pakistani, and much of the cooking was in their traditional style. Indian food had always been one of my favourites, so I was delighted to be able to enjoy it and learn more about it. But I also wanted to learn about the customs and styles of Arabic cooking, and I set about finding out what I could and experimenting in the kitchen.

Thus began my interest in Arabic food, and the more I learned, the more I wanted to know about this fascinating style of cooking, so sophisticated and entertaining. I decided to start lessons in both the language and the cooking, and it was during the cookery lessons that the idea of an Arabic cookery book surfaced. There were many young Westerners staying or living in Dubai, some married to Arabic men, who were trying to learn about Arab culture with no idea of the food and style of cooking, the spices used, or how the food was prepared and eaten.

7

One especially interesting point was that many households would not have an oven as nearly all the food is prepared on the stove top. If an oven was necessary, then the village might have a large communal oven which could be used.

When trying a new recipe it could be quite difficult to find all the ingredients. On one occasion when camping in the mountains, there was an Arabic family not far off. When it was expedient, I wandered over to where the ladies were sitting on their carpets preparing the food. If language was a complete barrier, then they would show me the ingredients used for that particular dish. They were always very hospitable and very pleased about my interest.

I hope you will enjoy the sophisticated and wonderful style of Arabic cooking as I do, and savour the whole new taste experience it opens up to you.

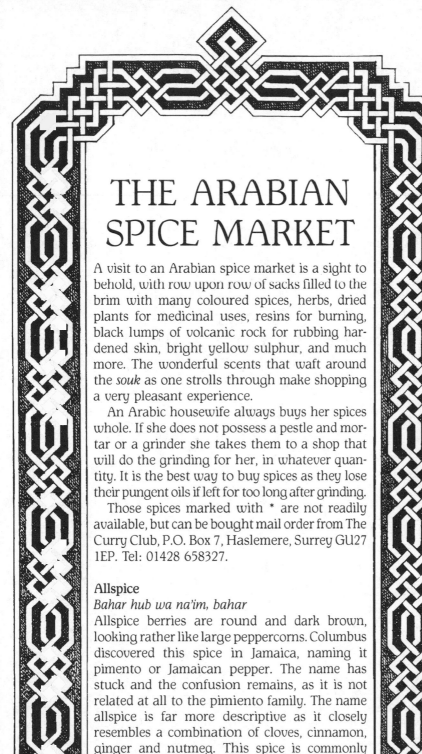

THE ARABIAN SPICE MARKET

A visit to an Arabian spice market is a sight to behold, with row upon row of sacks filled to the brim with many coloured spices, herbs, dried plants for medicinal uses, resins for burning, black lumps of volcanic rock for rubbing hardened skin, bright yellow sulphur, and much more. The wonderful scents that waft around the *souk* as one strolls through make shopping a very pleasant experience.

An Arabic housewife always buys her spices whole. If she does not possess a pestle and mortar or a grinder she takes them to a shop that will do the grinding for her, in whatever quantity. It is the best way to buy spices as they lose their pungent oils if left for too long after grinding.

Those spices marked with * are not readily available, but can be bought mail order from The Curry Club, P.O. Box 7, Haslemere, Surrey GU27 1EP. Tel: 01428 658327.

Allspice
Bahar hub wa na'im, bahar
Allspice berries are round and dark brown, looking rather like large peppercorns. Columbus discovered this spice in Jamaica, naming it pimento or Jamaican pepper. The name has stuck and the confusion remains, as it is not related at all to the pimiento family. The name allspice is far more descriptive as it closely resembles a combination of cloves, cinnamon, ginger and nutmeg. This spice is commonly referred to as *bahar* in the Middle East.

9

Anise
Yansoon
Small greyish-green seeds that were first cultivated in Egypt. They are used in savoury and sweet dishes.

Barberry
Zereshk
Reddish brown berries resembling currants when dried. They are very sour and used mainly by Iranians when cooking.

Bay leaf
Warak al gar
Green, spear-shaped leaves that are used the world over to add flavour to soups and stews. The leaf can be used straight from the tree or, more usually, in the dried form.

Blue poppy seeds
Bazour Zahrat
The primary use of poppy seeds in Arabic cookery is for garnishing breads and cakes; in ancient times the Egyptians used to feed their athletes on honey and poppy seed cakes in the belief that their strength and endurance would be increased.

Caraway
Karawya
Small, thin, dark grey seeds that have been used for centuries as a cooking spice in pastries, savouries, sweets and vegetables.

Cassia
Darseen
and
Cinnamon
Kirfee
These two are together in this glossary as they are so similar and do, from time to time, cause some confusion. They are closely related and both come from the inner bark of an evergreen tree, but from different species, cassia originating from China and cinnamon from Sri Lanka. Cinnamon is considered the better quality and is more generally used. It is an essential ingredient of *Baharat*.

Cloves
Habahan
Dark brown, nail-shaped dried flower bud of an evergreen tree. The clove is very widely used throughout the world, and in the 18th century it was used to ward off the bad smells of unwashed people. Cloves were stuck into an orange, covering it completely, cinnamon was then rubbed in and it was left to dry. The result was called a 'pomander' and these were hung in cupboards

and carried in little bags. These are still popular today. The clove is an important spice in all Eastern cooking.

Coriander (Cilantro)
Kazbara
These are round, pale brown seeds that are almost always used in the ground form; however, the fresh leaves are also used and these have a totally different flavour. This spice is also part of *Baharat*.

Cumin
Kamoon
Small, pale greenish seeds, a native of Egypt, but now widely used in most countries, usually in powder form.

Fenugreek
Hilbeh or hulbah
Golden brown, very hard rectangular seeds that have a rather bitter flavour that is lessened with cooking. It is an essential ingredient for the dried spiced beef dish *pastourma*, and is also used in Indian curries.

Ginger
Zanjabil
This is an irregularly shaped rhizome, with a thin skin that needs removing before use. The root will keep well for a long time in dry conditions. It is an essential part of Indian cookery. It is also used extensively for cakes and desserts in the west.

Green cardamom
Hayl or *hell* or *hail*
A green pod containing aromatic black seeds. These should be freshly ground to obtain the full flavour. This spice is a necessary ingredient for Arabic coffee. Cardamom is perhaps the second most expensive spice there is, but it is used throughout the Eastern world.

*Loomi
Also called noomi, these are limes that have been dried in the sun or in the case of Thailand dried on the trees. There are many Arabic dishes that include the loomi, but it is necessary to pierce it twice with a skewer before adding it to the food. A fresh lime or lemon can be used instead but the flavour is slightly different.

*Mahlab
This spice does not have an English equivalent as it is only found in the Middle East. It is the ground up kernel of the black cherry, though it is only bought whole as it loses its aromatic properties if kept in powder form. It is used in the baking of certain Arabic cakes and breads. Try using a few drops of almond essence (extract) instead, but its flavour will not be the same.

Nutmeg
Josat al teeb or *jawaz a'tib*
This is the kernel of the fruit of a tropical tree and is a very hard brown ball; it is used all over the world and is another important ingredient of *Baharat*.

Paprika
Filfil hilu
This is made from the ripened capsicum (bell) peppers, ground into a powder. The Arabic words when translated literally mean 'pepper sweet'. It is used equally for its flavour and colour.

Pomegranate
Ruman
A fruit known from ancient times and used in many forms. It is eaten fresh or the juice is extracted from the pulpy seeds and used in cooking; the juice is also made into Grenadine. The whole seeds are used as a colourful garnish for many types of food.

The pomegranate was a most respected fruit and at Turkish weddings the ripe fruit was thrown to the ground and the spilt seeds were counted; the result was a forecast of the number of children the couple would have.

Saffron
Za'faran
Saffron is the dried stigmas of the crocus plant. As there are only three to each plant and it takes some 75,000 hand-picked to produce 450 g/1 lb, this explains why saffron is the world's most expensive spice! The flavour is delicate and should not undergo a long cooking process. It imparts a strong yellow colour to any food.

Sesame seeds
Simsum
The seeds are pale yellow and come from a tropical tree, they are oily and are highly nutritious. Tahini paste is made from sesame seeds, and they are also used on breads and cakes. When using sesame oil the long cooking needed in stews helps to sweeten the flavour.

*Simen or Samneh
This is clarified butter and is usually made from sheep's or goat's milk, occasionally camel's. If it is made from cow's milk there is almost no difference from the Indian *ghee*. The great advantage of using *samneh* is that it can be heated to a higher temperature than other oils.

*Sumak
These are red berries that have been dried and ground to a coarse powder which has a slightly sour, lemony flavour.

Tamarind
Shar or *tamar hindi*
Tamarind is an Arabic word meaning 'the date of India'. It is a large bean pod from a tropical tree and is very acid; it is this aspect that is favoured by the Arabs and Indians. Before use, the pods need soaking in hot water for 10–15 minutes, then strained and the liquid used.

Turmeric
Kurkum
A rhizome which is ground to a fine dark yellow powder. Its primary use is for colouring but it does have a slightly bitter flavour, so do use sparingly. It is an important spice in curries.

*Zaatar
An Arabic word meaning thyme but it is bought as a blend of herbs and spices; it usually includes roasted sesame seeds, thyme, marjoram and *sumak*. Mixed with a little oil and spread on *khoubiz* before baking, it gives a spicy flavour to the bread. It can be used as flavouring for meat dishes.

Spice Mixtures
The following recipes are for spice mixtures that you will find in some of the recipes in this book. Grind a small batch and store in a screw top jar as the spices will lose their pungency if kept too long.

Lightly Spiced Salt
This is a light, aromatic salt.

100 g / 4 oz / ½ cup sea salt	5 ml / 1 tsp cinnamon
5 ml / 1 tsp allspice	

Mix the salt and spices together and store in a screw top jar.

Spicy Aromatic Salt
Stronger and spicier, this will also impart a delicate colour to food.

30 ml / 2 tbsp lightly spiced salt	2.5 ml / ½ tsp turmeric
5 ml / 1 tsp dried mint	2.5 ml / ½ tsp ground fenugreek
15 ml / 1 tbsp ground almonds	

Mix the ingredients together and store in a screw top jar.

Baharat

This widely used spice mixture varies from family to family and region to region. The following proportions are the most usual.

90 ml / 6 tbsp black peppercorns	45 ml / 3 tbsp cloves
45 ml / 3 tbsp coriander (cilantro) seeds	60 ml / 4 tbsp cumin seeds
45 ml / 3 tbsp broken cinnamon or cassia sticks	10 ml / 2 tsp cardamom seeds
	2 whole nutmegs
	90 ml / 6 tbsp paprika

1   Grind all the spices, except the nutmeg and paprika. Grate the nutmegs and add with the paprika to the mixture.

2   Store in a screw top jar in a cool, dark place.

La Kama

This spice mixture from Tangier in Morocco is especially popular for flavouring stews and soups.

30 ml / 2 tbsp ground black pepper	15 ml / 1 tbsp turmeric
30 ml / 2 tbsp ground ginger	15 ml / 1 tbsp cinnamon
.5 ml / 1 tsp nutmeg	

Mix together and store in a screw top jar in a cool, dark place.

MEZZA
HORS D'OEUVRES

When the Arabs roamed the desserts from oasis to oasis looking for grazing ground for their animals or travelling the spice routes, then hospitality to a lone traveller, friend or neighbour could mean the difference between life and death. It might take the form of tea or coffee served in tiny cups, a cooling yoghurt drink or fruit juices. It might also be accompanied by morsels of food such as dates or olives. So it is, perhaps, from these small beginnings that the *mezza* has grown to such enormous proportions that now the variety is endless. There could be as many as 40 dishes served for a special occasion. They span an array of countless colours, textures and flavours.

When presenting the food it should be in small portions arranged decoratively on a plate. The dips are put into special *mezza* type bowls made of earthenware, usually with one or two wide splashes of a cream slip. An abundance of Arabic bread is always served with the meal. Using only the right hand, the bread is broken into small pieces and used to pick up the food.

The *mezza* should contain as wide an assortment of food as possible: a selection of dips and many types of salads, the diverse shapes and flavours of *kibbeh* (ground meat and cracked wheat), slices of tongue, also, perhaps, finger-size sausages, little pieces of squid and tiny fried fish, cheese laid out in slices on a flat dish, and

15

small cubes of fried cheese and olives, stuffed vegetables, such as the potato and burghul balls and/or vine and cabbage leaves with a variety of fillings. Small pickles, such as pickled aubergines (eggplants), are also served to add colour to the table and a richness to the food. Yoghurt will always be included, either as a dip or a sauce to be eaten with other foods.

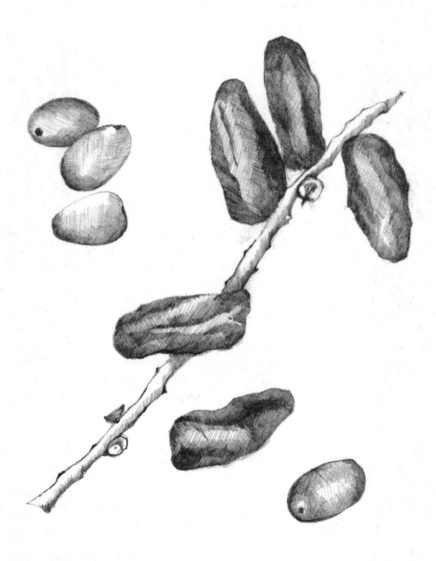

MUJADARAH
Rice and Lentil Pilaff

S erved warm, Mujadara *is a delicious dish in its own right.* *However, it would also make an unusual accompaniment to a main course.*

◄§ S E R V E S 4 - 6 §►

350 g / 12 oz / 2 cups brown lentils	4 large onions
12.5 ml / 2½ tsp salt	100 g / 4 oz / ½ cup risotto rice
Oil for frying	

1   Wash and cook the lentils in plenty of boiling water with 5 ml/1 tsp salt until they are soft. Drain, reserving the liquid. Sieve or process, adding enough liquid to make a soft but not runny purée.

2   Finely chop 2 of the onions, fry (sauté) them in 30 ml/2 tbsp oil until they are light yellow, then drain them on kitchen paper.

3   Put the puréed lentils, fried onions and the rice with the remaining salt in a large pan, add enough water to cover them and cook slowly, stirring from time to time until the *mujadarah* becomes thick. More liquid may be added if necessary. It should be similar to a thick porridge.

4   Slice the remaining onions and fry them in 45 ml/3 tbsp hot oil until they are brown and crisp.

5   To serve, pour the *mujadarah* on to a flat plate and garnish with the crisply fried onions.

HUMMUS-BI-TAHINI
Hummus with Tahini

Hummus-bi-tahini *and* Baba Ghannouj *are very similar in so far as the flavourings of tahini and lemon juice are used in both. A small dish of this is very often served as part of a meal in many Arabic restaurants and tiny cafés. As when eating* Baba Ghannouj, *small leaves of Cos lettuce or pieces of Arabic bread are used to scoop up the hummus.*

It was from my Arabic neighbour that I learned the value of using freshly cooked dried chick peas rather than the tinned variety I had been using.

This may also be frozen successfully; defrost as for Baba Ghannouj.

◦§ SERVES 4–6 §◦

1 lb / 450 g / 2⅔ cups chick peas (garbanzos) soaked in cold water overnight	GARNISH
3 garlic cloves, crushed	Olive oil
300 ml / ½ pt / 1¼ cups tahini	Paprika
30–45 ml / 2–3 tbsp lemon juice	Black olives
	10 ml / 2 tsp salt

1 Drain the chick peas then place in a large pan and cover with cold water, bring to the boil and simmer for about 1–1½ hours until the chick peas are tender, removing the scum when necessary. Do not add salt at this stage. If you have a pressure cooker the cooking time will be greatly reduced.

2 Drain the chick peas, reserving 250 ml/8 fl oz/1 cup of the liquid and a few whole chick peas for garnishing.

3 Purée the chick peas and garlic in a blender, or use a potato masher. Add some of the cooking liquid if the purée is too thick.

4 Add the tahini and lemon juice alternately, beating between each addition. The finished purée should be of a creamy consistency. Taste for seasoning.

5   Serve in small bowls or on a large flat dish. Smooth the hummus
    with the back of a spoon making a shallow depression in an inner
    circle round the bowl. Fill this with a little olive oil. Add a sprinkling
    of paprika, then arrange the reserved chick peas decoratively on the
    hummus. A black olive placed in the centre adds an attractive
    contrasting colour.

LABAN BI TUM
Yoghurt Dip

*T*his delicious dip is a must to serve with mezza. It should be
well chilled before serving to be at its refreshing best.

◆§ S E R V E S 4 – 6 §◆

450 ml / ¾ pt / 2 cups natural (plain) yoghurt	2.5 ml / ½ tsp salt
1–2 garlic cloves	15 ml / 1 tbsp chopped fresh mint
	A few mint leaves to garnish

1   Beat the yoghurt until creamy.

2   Pound the garlic with the salt and add to the yoghurt with the
    chopped mint.

3   Put into 1 or 2 small bowls and garnish with whole mint leaves.
    Chill well before serving.

BABA GHANNOUJ
Aubergine Dip

Baba Ghannouj, *also called Mutabel, is a delightfully tangy dip which is almost a must for any mezza table. It is traditionally eaten with Arabic or pitta bread, but you can try vegetables such as sticks of celery, carrots or small lettuce leaves.*

The secret of making this delicious dish is the smoking of the aubergine. This can be done by holding it against a gas flame and turning it frequently until the inside flesh is soft. Apart from resting the aubergines on a barbecue grid there is no other method that can produce that authentic smoky flavour. However, you will be able to produce a tasty baba ghannouj *by placing the aubergines in a hot oven or under a hot grill (broiler) until the skins are black and the flesh is soft. The flavour should be an equal balance between those of the aubergine, tahini and lemon juice.*

This dish may be frozen. When defrosting, transfer to the fridge overnight. Beat the dip well before serving.

⋅§ SERVES 4-6 §⋅

2 large aubergines (eggplants)	60 ml / 4 tbsp lemon juice
3 garlic cloves	15 ml / 1 tbsp olive oil
5 ml / 1 tsp salt	1 black olive
60 ml / 4 tbsp tahini	Arabic bread or vegetable sticks to serve

1 Cook the aubergines over a gas flame, turning them frequently until the skins are black and the inside flesh is soft.

2 Peel the skin off the aubergines, taking care to remove all the charred particles. Mash or beat the flesh to a smooth paste.

3 Crush the garlic with the salt then add to the aubergines. Add the tahini and lemon juice alternately, mixing thoroughly after each addition. Adjust the proportions of tahini, lemon juice and salt to taste.

4 Pour the *baba ghannouj* into a shallow bowl or a flat dish. Using the back of a spoon, make a narrow depression in an inner circle around the bowl, fill this with a ribbon of olive oil and place a black olive in the centre. Serve with Arabic bread or vegetable sticks.

HILBEH
Hot Fenugreek Dip

*F*enugreek seeds form the basis for this dip that is native to the southern Arabian Gulf. It can be very bitter unless the seeds are first soaked overnight.

◄§ SERVES 4 - 6 §►

30 ml / 2 tbsp fenugreek seeds, soaked overnight	30 ml / 2 tbsp chopped fresh coriander (cilantro)
1 large onion, chopped	3-4 tomatoes, chopped
4-8 garlic cloves, crushed	2-3 green chillies, finely chopped
30 ml / 2 tbsp olive oil	45 ml / 3 tbsp lemon juice
5 ml / 1 tsp baharat (page 14)	Arabic bread to serve

1 Drain the fenugreek seeds well.

2 Fry (sauté) the onions and garlic in the oil and add the strained seeds. Continue to fry for a minute or two, then add the baharat and coriander, frying for a further 3 minutes.

3 Place the mixture in a blender with the tomatoes, chillies and lemon juice, and blend until a thick purée forms.

4 To serve pour the mixture into a small bowl and serve with Arabic bread.

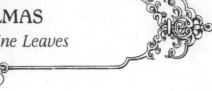

DOLMAS
Stuffed Vine Leaves

*T*hese delicious tiny stuffed vine leaves are another part of the
mezza which is becoming increasingly popular in Western
restaurants. I was once served these at a banquet in Sharjah where
the centre piece was a whole cooked lamb surrounded by a low
'wall' of these delicious dolmas; the flavour of the rice and the vine
leaves was quite delightful.

◄§ SERVES 4–6 §►

225 g / 8 oz vine leaves	30 ml / 2 tbsp chopped parsley
225 g / 8 oz / 1 cup risotto rice	30 ml / 2 tbsp chopped mint
1 onion, finely chopped	2.5 ml / ½ tsp allspice
1 garlic clove, crushed	30 ml / 2 tbsp lemon juice
30 ml / 2 tbsp olive oil	30 ml / 2 tbsp tomato purée (paste)

Chopped lettuce to serve

1   Blanch the vine leaves in boiling water for 2 minutes, then rinse
    under cold water and remove any tough stems.

2   Wash, soak and drain the rice then lightly fry (sauté) it with the
    onion and garlic in the oil. Add 300 ml/½ pt/1¼ cups water and
    bring to the boil. Simmer the rice until all the liquid has been
    absorbed. The rice should not be completely cooked at this stage.

3   Add the parsley, mint and allspice and mix gently together.

4   Place 1 leaf at a time right side down on a board. Put about 15 ml/
    1 tbsp of the filling at the base of the leaf then fold in the sides and
    roll up into a little parcel. Do not roll them too tightly as the rice
    will expand further.

5   Any left over or broken leaves can be used to line a shallow pan
    with a well-fitting lid.

6   Place the dolmas in the pan seam side down, packing them closely
    together.

7   Mix the lemon juice and tomato purée with enough water to cover
    the dolmas well. Place a plate on top to prevent any movement and
    cover with a lid.

8   Cook gently on low heat until all the liquid has been absorbed,
    leaving the dolmas in the pan to cool.

9   Serve on a bed of chopped lettuce.

Variations
- Burghul may replace the rice, giving a pleasant nutty flavour.

- An alternative presentation. Instead of putting the dolmas in a single
  layer, use a straight sided pan with a well fitting lid. Line the base
  with the left over leaves, then on top of these place slices of
  decoratively cut potatoes. Then place the dolmas so that they are
  piled 10 cm/3–4 in high. These are then cooked in the same way.
  When the cooking has finished and they are cold place a clean plate
  over the dolmas and turn the pan upside down. You now have a
  mound of dolmas with the decorative potatoes on top. Garnish with
  slices of radish or tomatoes.

FALAFEL
Fried Bean Croquettes

*T*his dish is claimed by both Egypt and Israel as their national dish, though there is evidence that both the Pharaohs and their slaves enjoyed these delightful little 'cakes'. The Israelis used chick peas (garbanzos) as they were more easily obtained, whereas the Egyptians used dried green broad (lima) beans. This recipe uses both.

On almost any street in the east can be found a small stall selling these dark brown crispy bean croquettes. The mixture is scraped up and put into a special brass falafel mould, smoothed over and then popped out and into hot oil to deep fry until crisp. They can be seen arranged around a heavy cast iron black wok called a sajjah, just waiting to be bought. A bag of these crunchy snacks costs only a few pence. They may also be sold broken up and mixed with tomatoes, mint leaves and lettuce, all packed into a pocket of Arabic bread.

These are not difficult to make at home and many variations are open to the imaginative cook.

◆§ SERVES 4 – 6 §◆

225 g / 8 oz / 1⅓ cups chick peas (garbanzos), soaked overnight and cooked	60 ml / 4 tbsp chopped parsley
225 g / 8 oz / 1⅓ cups dried green broad (lima) beans, soaked overnight and cooked	30 ml / 2 tbsp chopped fresh coriander (cilantro)
4 garlic cloves, crushed	5-10 ml / 1-2 tsp ground coriander seed (cilantro)
4 onions, very finely chopped	5 ml / 1 tsp ground cumin
	Salt and pepper
Oil for deep frying	

1 Mash the cooked chick peas and broad beans to a fairly firm paste. Add all the remaining ingredients.

2 Mix the paste thoroughly and leave it to stand for 30 minutes. If the paste will not hold together add 30-45 ml/2-3 tbsp plain (all-purpose) flour.

3   Form into small flat rounds and deep fry (sauté) them until they are
    brown and crisp. Drain on kitchen paper.

Variation
*   Cooked mashed potatoes, chopped nuts or caraway seeds may be
    added for more variety.

SARDALYA TAVASI
Fried Sardines

F reshly caught fish are one of the delights of an Arab souk.
    However, your local supermarket should also be able to provide
fresh sardines for this quick but tasty dish.

SERVES 4 – 6

1 kg / 2 lb sardines, washed and cleaned	1 egg, beaten with 15 ml / 1 tbsp milk
Plain (all-purpose) flour for coating	Oil for frying
Salt and pepper	Lemon or lime slices

1   Coat the fish in the flour, seasoned with salt and pepper.

2   Dip the coated fish into the egg mixture then cover them again with
    the flour.

3   Heat the oil in a deep pan then fry (sauté) the fish a few at a time
    until they are crisp. Drain them on kitchen paper.

4   Serve the sardines with slices of lemon or lime.

AL KABBA BILBORGHOL
Potato and Burghul Balls

*T*hese patties will be favoured by vegetarians as they do not contain meat or fish. The quantity of herbs and spices may be varied according to taste.

◆§ SERVES 4–6 §◆

6 potatoes, peeled and quartered	1.5 ml /¼ tsp allspice
175 g / 6 oz / 1½ cups fine burghul wheat	75 ml / 5 tbsp pine nuts
Salt and pepper	60 ml / 4 tbsp raisins
FILLING	45 ml / 3 tbsp tahini paste
2 onions, finely chopped	A little plain (all-purpose) flour
1 garlic clove, crushed	Salad to serve

1   Boil the potatoes until tender. Drain and mash them.

2   Just cover the burghul with boiling water and leave to stand for 15 minutes. Combine with the potatoes, and salt and pepper to taste. Mix to a paste.

3   For the filling: fry (sauté) the onions in the oil until they are brown, add the garlic and all the remaining ingredients, mixing well together, then adjust the seasoning.

4   With wet hands shape a spoonful of the potato paste into a ball then flatten it into a disc. Place a spoonful of the filling into the centre. Mould the paste around the filling into a smooth oval, roll in a little flour and chill for 30 minutes.

5   Deep fry until golden brown and drain on kitchen paper.

6   Serve hot or cold with salad.

KIBDAH MALEYAH
Sautéed Liver

*T*he liver of sheep, goats or chicken is cooked in many ways throughout the Arabic world. In Tunisia and the Yemen it is spicy and fiery hot, in Qatar they use an abundance of garlic, while in Morocco they flavour their cooking oil with paprika, coriander (cilantro) and cumin prior to cooking the liver. Whichever method you choose it is a quick and simple dish full of nutrients.

◆§ SERVES 4 §◆

350 g / 12 oz lambs' or chicken liver	Oil for frying
150 g / 5 oz / 1¼ cups plain (all-purpose) flour	GARNISH
15-30 ml / 1-2 tbsp baharat (page 14)	Sprigs of coriander (cilantro) or parsley
Salt and pepper	Lemon wedges

1 Wash the liver and remove any large veins, then cut into small strips.

2 Mix the flour, baharat, salt and pepper and coat the pieces of liver.

3 Stir-fry the liver in hot oil until evenly browned. It should still be slightly pink inside. Do not overcook the liver as this will make it tough.

4 Serve hot garnished with the coriander or parsley and a lemon wedge for each person.

KIBBEH
Stuffed Meatballs

*I*n the fertile areas of Syria, Jordan and the Lebanon the art of making these stuffed spicy meatballs in their varied shapes and sizes has been practised to perfection.

In our village there was one woman whom we called the 'Kibbeh maker' as she was said to have 'Kibbeh fingers' (rather like a gardener's green ones). To eat one meat ball in a couple of bites is not nearly long enough to gain appreciation for the art of making kibbeh. However, it can be mastered with time and patience. The use of a food processor greatly reduces the time taken in grinding and mincing the ingredients.

There are many variations of the kibbeh and the amount of spices that are used is very much according to taste. Kibbeh may be prepared ahead of time and frozen.

In the Arab world they prefer to use the pink flesh of the yearling lamb, but older lamb or beef may be substituted.

◦§ SERVES 4–6 §◦

CASING	FILLING
225 g / 8 oz / 1½ cups burghul	1 onion, finely chopped
450 g / 1 lb lean lamb, finely minced (ground)	15 ml / 1 tbsp oil
1 large onion, sliced	225 g / 8 oz / 2 cups lamb, minced (ground)
Salt and pepper	50 g / 2 oz / ½ cup pine nuts
	2.5 ml / ½ tsp cinnamon
	2.5 ml / ½ allspice

1 To make the casing: put the burghul into a bowl and pour over enough boiling water to cover. Stand for 15 minutes to absorb the water.

2 Put the burghul, lamb and onion in a food processor and blend to a paste, then add a little salt and pepper.

3   Prepare the filling: fry (sauté) the onion in the oil then add the lamb
    and half the pine nuts. Cook over a gentle heat for 3 minutes,
    stirring until part-cooked, but not brown. Add a little water to soften
    and add the spices and cook for a further 2 minutes.

4   Smooth half the casing mixture on to an oiled baking dish. Layer the
    filling on top, spreading it evenly over the casing. Then finish with
    the remaining casing mixture.

5   Make shallow cuts of diagonal lines criss-crossing the meat. Place a
    pine nut in the centre of each diamond. Brush a little oil over the
    surface.

6   Bake at 160°C/325°F/gas mark 3 for 1 hour or until brown and crisp
    on top.

Variations

*   To make small oval kibbeh for a *mezza* make up to step 3 then:

4   Divide the casing mixture into 10 or 12 equal portions.

5   With wet hands take a small portion of the casing mixture and
    smooth into a ball. Hollow the inside by pushing a thumb into the
    centre of the ball. Pinch the sides while rolling the ball around the
    palm of your hand. This 'potter's action' is continued until a round
    thin shell is formed.

6   Put 5 ml/1 tsp of the filling into each shell and close the walls
    around it. Smooth over and chill for 30 minutes before cooking.

7   Deep fry for 6-8 minutes or until deep brown. Drain them on kitchen
    paper.

*   An Iraqi version contains almonds and raisins instead of the pine
    nuts, and the mixture is shaped into flat discs.

MUMBAR
Lamb Sausage

*T*his is a strongly flavoured, spiced sausage that is really not
difficult to make. The sausage casing is pushed on to the end of
a large funnel resting over a jug. The meat can then be pushed
down the funnel and so into the skin, tying knots between each
sausage according to the size required. You can buy simple sausage-
making machines from good kitchen shops. There are many
variations of mumbar throughout the Middle East. The sausages
can be served as part of the mezza or as a main course, when they
could be larger.

SERVES 4-6

675 g / 1½ lb / 3 cups lamb or beef coarsely minced (ground)	30 ml /2 tbsp chopped parsley
6-8 garlic cloves, crushed	200 g / 7 oz / scant cup basmati rice, washed
1 small onion, finely chopped	Salt and pepper
5 ml / 1 tsp barahat (page 14)	2 m / 6 ft thick sausage casing
90 ml / 6 tbsp olive oil	Stock

1 Mix all the ingredients together, except the sausage casing and the
stock.

2 If you do not have a machine for filling the skins then use a large
funnel. Feed the skins over the end of the funnel, pushing on as
much as you can. Put the meat in the top of the funnel, pushing
gently down and so into the skins. Tie a knot between each sausage.
Fill them as evenly as you can by running wet hands down the
length of the filled skins.

3 Place the coiled sausages into a pan and cover with well-flavoured
stock. Gently bring them to the boil and simmer them slowly for 1
hour. Leave them to cool in the pan with whatever liquid is left.

4 They may be served hot or cold, cut into lengths or sliced.

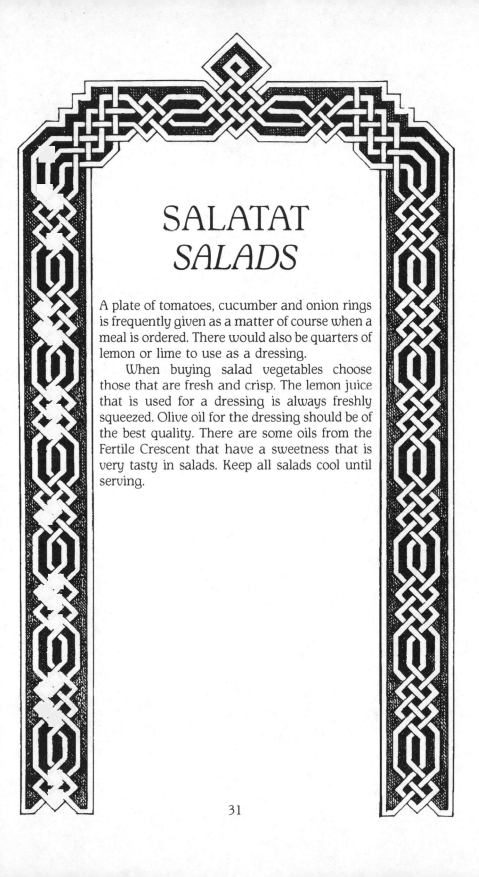

SALATAT
SALADS

A plate of tomatoes, cucumber and onion rings is frequently given as a matter of course when a meal is ordered. There would also be quarters of lemon or lime to use as a dressing.

When buying salad vegetables choose those that are fresh and crisp. The lemon juice that is used for a dressing is always freshly squeezed. Olive oil for the dressing should be of the best quality. There are some oils from the Fertile Crescent that have a sweetness that is very tasty in salads. Keep all salads cool until serving.

SALATA MUTANANIA TAZIJA
Fresh Herbs Salad

*T*he Arabs have a great liking for simple herbs, so a dish of these with a few whole salad ingredients are put on the table and left there to be nibbled at throughout the meal. Listed is a sample version of a collection of herbs and vegetables.

Cos lettuce leaves	Bunch of radishes
Watercress	5-6 leaves of spinach
Sprigs of mint, coriander (cilantro) and basil	Bunch of parsley
1 cucumber	1 green (bell) pepper
	1-2 tomatoes

1 Wash and carefully dry a selection of herbs and vegetables.

2 Arrange decoratively on a large oval plate and serve without dressing.

LISANAT MATABBLE
Lamb Tongue Salad

L ambs' tongues are available from butchers and some supermarkets. The meat is tender and succulent. For a quick alternative use ready cooked pressed lambs' tongue, either canned or from the delicatessen counter.

◄§ SERVES 4 - 6 §►

5 lambs' tongues	60 ml / 4 tbsp olive oil
2 garlic cloves, crushed	GARNISH
15 ml / 1 tbsp salt	30 ml / 2 tbsp finely chopped parsley
75 ml / 5 tbsp lemon juice	

1   Wash the tongues and simmer in water with 1 garlic clove and salt for 1 hour until tender.

2   Remove the skin and gristle and slice the meat.

3   Mix the lemon juice with the oil and remaining garlic, pour over the tongues and leave to marinate for a short time.

4   Garnish with the parsley.

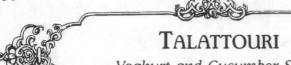

TALATTOURI
Yoghurt and Cucumber Salad

*T*his combination of yoghurt and cucumber is made in many countries. In India it is called raita. It is possible that it was the Indians who first introduced that particular mixture to the Arabs. It is only fairly recently that cucumbers have been grown in the UAE. This and the following Spinach and Yoghurt Salad are a most cooling and refreshing addition to any meal. Serve both well chilled in small bowls.

 SERVES 4–6

1 large or 2 small cucumbers	Salt and pepper to taste
300 ml / ½ pt / 1¼ cups natural (plain) yoghurt	GARNISH
30 ml / 2 tbsp chopped mint	Sprigs of mint

1   If you wish, the cucumber may be peeled, but I prefer the peel to remain on as it adds to the flavour and colour of the completed dish. Chop the cucumber into small cubes.

2   Add the chopped cucumber to the yoghurt with the mint, mixing well and adjusting the seasoning. Garnish with sprigs of mint.

Variation:
- If a thicker yoghurt is preferred it may be put into a cloth to hang for an hour, by which time some of the whey will have dripped out. Beat well before adding the cucumber. A well crushed clove of garlic may be added.

SALATET SABENEG-BIL LEBAN
Spinach and Yoghurt Salad

*L*ightly toasted crushed walnuts can be sprinkled over the top of this refreshing salad.

•§ SERVES 4 - 6 §•

450 g / 1 lb spinach	Salt and pepper to taste
1 onion, chopped	GARNISH
1-2 garlic cloves, crushed	Sprigs of mint
30 ml / 2 tbsp olive oil	
300 ml / ½ pt / 1¼ cups natural (plain) yoghurt	

1 Wash the spinach in plenty of water and remove the stalks. Drain the leaves well and then roughly chop them.

2 Lightly fry (sauté) the onion and garlic in the oil until soft, add the spinach and continue to cook until the spinach softens. Allow this to cool.

3 Combine the spinach with the yoghurt, season and chill.

4 Garnish with sprigs of mint.

TABOULEH
Burghul Wheat Salad

Tabouleh *was once considered a dish that was native to the mountainous areas of the Lebanon, but such was its popularity that it soon spread throughout the Middle East. In the past burghul was a staple grain always available and cheap, so in many households, where vegetables were scarce, the grain predominated. In more fertile areas, where salad ingredients were readily available, the proportions were strongly in favour of vegetables and herbs. It is still a highly debated recipe, with each household having their own preference, so do experiment with this delicious salad to find the proportions of grain to vegetables that will suit your family.*

◆§ SERVES 4-6 §◆

100 g / 4 oz / 1 cup fine burghul	DRESSING
175 ml / 6 fl oz / ¾ cup boiling water	1 garlic clove, crushed
5 ml / 1 tsp salt	90 ml / 6 tbsp lemon juice
3 large tomatoes, skinned and finely chopped	90 ml / 6 tbsp olive oil
60 ml / 4 tbsp chopped mint	GARNISH
60 ml / 4 tbsp chopped parsley	Lettuce leaves and sprigs of mint

1   Put the burghul into a bowl and cover it with the boiling salted water. Leave it to stand for 15 minutes until all the water has been absorbed.

2   Mix the dressing ingredients together and pour over the burghul. This can now be refrigerated until the following day, by which time the flavours of the dressing will have been absorbed.

3   Put the chopped tomatoes, mint and parsley into a large bowl and add the burghul.

4   To serve, arrange the lettuce leaves around the edge of a serving dish and pile the salad in the centre. Garnish with sprigs of mint.

JIBNAH MALIAH
Fried Cheese and Olives

The best cheeses for frying are the firm blocks similar to the Greek feta and the Cypriot haloumi, both available here. Avoid cheeses which melt easily.

◅§ S E R V E S 6 §▻

225 g / 8 oz firm white cheese	10-15 black olives
Olive oil for frying	Lemon juice

1 Cut the cheese into 1 cm/½ in cubes.

2 Heat the olive oil and add the cubes a few at a time, gently frying (sautéing) them until lightly brown on all sides.

3 Serve immediately with the black olives and a light sprinkling of lemon juice. Accompany with Arabic bread.

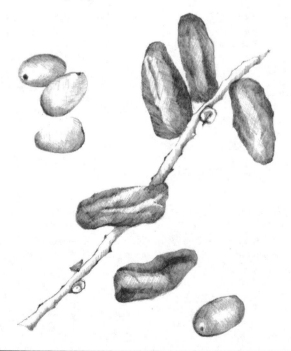

FATTOUSH
Mixed Salad

*F*attoush is a lovely salad of many ingredients and flavours, said to have originated in Syria. 'Fattoush', which literally means 'wet bread', was a unique way of using yesterday's bread.

The sumak is a crushed dried red berry which gives the salad a delightful colour and an unusual flavour (see page 12). An alternative would be to use a sprinkling of finely grated lemon rind and a dusting of paprika.

In the Arab world fattoush would vary in each region according to the availability of salad ingredients. In Egypt, for example, the dark green leaves of melokhia are tossed in, while others would use spinach leaves which are very similar.

Whole spring onions (scallions) and green chillies might be placed around the rim of the salad bowl.

◄§ SERVES 4 - 6 §►

4 large tomatoes, chopped	2 garlic cloves, crushed
4 cucumbers, chopped	120-250 ml / 4-8 fl oz / ½-1 cup lemon juice
2 large green (bell) peppers, chopped	125 ml / 4 fl oz / ½ cup olive oil
2 carrots, chopped	5 ml/1 tsp cinnamon
5 large radishes, chopped	Salt and pepper
1 large white onion, chopped	1 large Arabic bread, toasted
2 bunches of parsley, chopped	10 ml / 2 tsp sumak (page 12)
1 bunch of mint, chopped	

1   Put all the prepared vegetables into a deep bowl.

2   Add the crushed garlic to the lemon juice, add the oil and cinnamon, mix well then pour over the salad and mix gently. Taste for seasoning.

3   Put into a serving bowl and cover with Arabic bread toasted and broken into small pieces. Sprinkle the sumak over the salad and serve immediately.

BATATA BI KIZBARA
Potatoes with Coriander

*T*his is a fine example of the ingenuity of Arabic cooking. These ordinary fried potatoes are turned into an exotic dish that is quite delicious.

◆§ SERVES 4 - 6 §◆

Oil for deep frying	1 bunch of coriander (cilantro)
2 kg / 1 lb potatoes, peeled and cubed	Salt to taste
50-120 ml / 2-4 fl oz / ¼-½ cup lemon juice	50 g / 2 oz / ½ cup pine nuts, toasted
5 garlic cloves, crushed	

1   Heat enough oil to deep fry the potatoes, in two batches if necessary, until they are dark and golden. Place on kitchen paper to drain.

2   In another pan put the lemon juice, garlic and coriander. Add the potatoes, stir fry for 5 minutes. Season with salt.

3   Turn into a bowl and garnish with the toasted pine nuts. Serve warm.

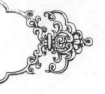

FUL MEDAMES
Beans with Eggs and Parsley

*O*n one memorable occasion whilst camping in the desert, among *the red gold sand dunes, we had finished our evening meal when a large* damassa *(Egyptian cooking pot) half filled with ful mesdames was set on the cooling embers. A few well scrubbed eggs were added to the pot. This was then left to cook all night long. The fire was replenished from time to time with the wood we had brought with us.*

As the sun came up we were each presented with a bowl of ful. The shelled eggs had been crumbled over the beans.

This famously delicious Eastern dish certainly lived up to its reputation. I shall never forget the romantic setting of the dunes, and the dawn, or the tall Arab in his long white kandoora who served us. I even forgave him for constantly disturbing my sleep as he tended his fire. This is the ideal dish to cook in an Aga or slow-cooker after an initial fast boil.

◆§ SERVES 4 §◆

450 g / 1 lb / 2 cups Egyptian brown (field) beans, soaked overnight	2.5 ml / ½ tsp pepper
3 garlic cloves, crushed	4 eggs, shells well scrubbed
30 ml / 2 tbsp olive oil	Juice of 2 lemons
5 ml / 1 tsp salt	30 ml / 2 tbsp finely chopped parsley

1 Drain the beans and put into a large heavy pan with plenty of water. Bring to the boil, boil rapidly for 10 minutes. Add the garlic, olive oil and the eggs. Cover and simmer on a very low heat for 6 hours or more until the beans are really tender.

2 Towards the end of the cooking time add the salt. Remove the eggs and shell and slice them.

3 To serve, place the beans into individual bowls with the egg slices on top of the beans. Either sprinkle with the lemon juice and parsley or hand around separately.

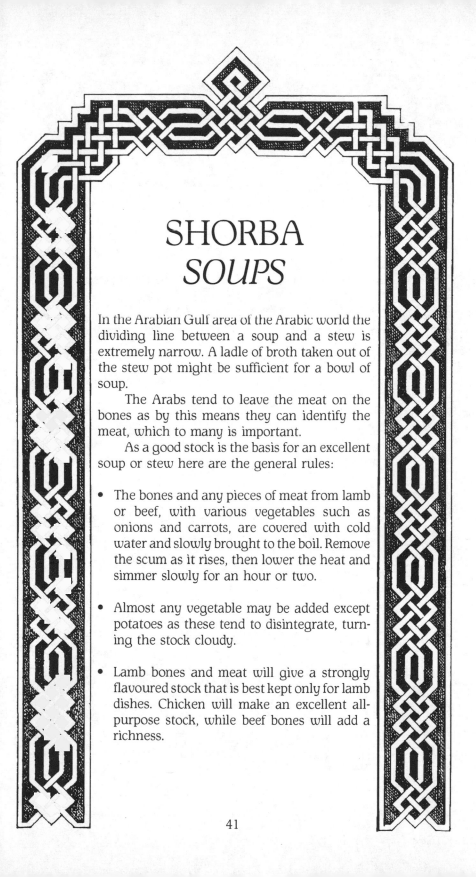

SHORBA
SOUPS

In the Arabian Gulf area of the Arabic world the dividing line between a soup and a stew is extremely narrow. A ladle of broth taken out of the stew pot might be sufficient for a bowl of soup.

The Arabs tend to leave the meat on the bones as by this means they can identify the meat, which to many is important.

As a good stock is the basis for an excellent soup or stew here are the general rules:

- The bones and any pieces of meat from lamb or beef, with various vegetables such as onions and carrots, are covered with cold water and slowly brought to the boil. Remove the scum as it rises, then lower the heat and simmer slowly for an hour or two.

- Almost any vegetable may be added except potatoes as these tend to disintegrate, turning the stock cloudy.

- Lamb bones and meat will give a strongly flavoured stock that is best kept only for lamb dishes. Chicken will make an excellent all-purpose stock, while beef bones will add a richness.

41

SHORBIT ADIS
Lentil Soup

A ny soup made from lentils is tasty and filling. The lemon gives a dash of piquancy to this wholesome soup.

◄§ SERVES 6-8 §►

450 g / 1 lb / 2 cups yellow lentils	Salt and pepper
1.75 l / 3 pts / 7½ cups stock	30 ml / 2 tbsp lemon juice
1 onion, quartered	Oil for frying
1 garlic clove, chopped	2 onions, sliced
1.5 ml / ¼ tsp cumin	Lemon wedges

1   Wash and drain the lentils, then cover them in the stock with the onion, garlic, cumin, salt and pepper. Bring to the boil, cover and simmer for 30-40 minutes. Purée if liked.

2   Add the lemon juice.

3   Fry the onions until crisp, and serve sprinkled over the soup with the lemon wedges on the side.

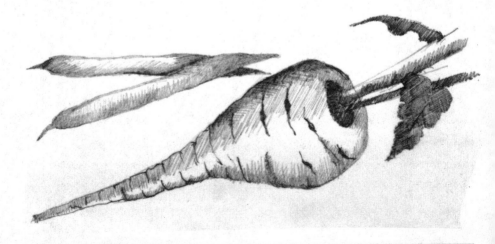

SHREET ADS MAJROOSH
Lentil Soup with Cumin

*C*umin *is a popular spice in Arabic cooking. It is used here to give a distinctive aromatic quality to a simple lentil soup.*

◆§ SERVES 6-8 §◆

450 g / 1 lb / 2 cups split red lentils	50 g / 2 oz / ¼ cup butter
1.75 l / 3 pts / 7½ cups stock or water	15 ml / 1 tbsp onion, chopped
1 onion, quartered	10 ml / 2 tsp ground cumin
1 tomato, quartered	5 ml / 1 tsp salt
1 stick (rib) of celery with leaves, chopped	1.5 ml / ¼ tsp pepper
1 garlic clove, chopped	GARNISH
	2 lemons, cut into wedges

1 Wash and drain the lentils.

2 Bring the stock or water to the boil in a large saucepan then add the lentils, quartered onion, tomato, celery and garlic; stir well. Bring back to the boil.

3 Reduce heat, cover and simmer for 30-45 minutes or until the lentils are tender.

4 Meanwhile, in a small pan, melt half the butter and fry the chopped onion until golden; set aside.

5 Purée the soup through a sieve or an electric blender.

6 Return the soup to the saucepan and cook for 5 minutes, stirring continuously, then add the cumin, salt and pepper. Just before serving add the remaining half of the butter. Serve with fried onions and a wedge of lemon for each person.

LOUHOUMAT KHODAR SOUPPA
Meat and Vegetable Soup

*T*he possibilities for this hearty soup are endless. Rich in
ingredients, it is almost a meal in itself. Various meat cuts as
well as an assortment of vegetables may be used to create this
substantial soup.

◄§ SERVES 6-8 §►

450 g / 1 lb stewing meat on the bone	3 tomatoes, chopped
1.75 l / 3 pts / 7½ cups stock	Pinch of cayenne pepper
1 large onion, roughly chopped	Salt and pepper
1-2 carrots, roughly chopped	GARNISH
2 potatoes, cut into quarters	Chopped parsley
Arabic bread to serve	

1   Put the meat and stock into a large pan with the vegetables and
bring slowly to the boil, removing the scum as it rises.

2   Add the cayenne, salt and pepper. Lower the heat and continue to
simmer the soup until the meat is well cooked. The bones can be
removed at this stage.

3   Add more stock if necessary, and adjust the seasoning.

4   Garnish with chopped parsley and serve with Arabic bread.

SHORBA DEJAJ
Chicken Soup

*A*s with most Arabic soups, this recipe can be adapted to make use of almost any seasonal vegetable – carrots, leeks, celery or green beans. There is an Egyptian version that uses celery, leeks and courgettes (zucchini) called Hamud.

    The Middle Eastern style of chicken soup, unlike its western counterpart, has a strongly aromatic flavour from the liberal use of lemon juice and garlic.

⋅§ SERVES 6 §⋅

1 onion, chopped	1–2 sticks (ribs) of celery, chopped
1–2 garlic cloves, crushed	Peas or beans
1.2 l / 2 pts / 5 cups chicken stock	3 cardamom pods, crushed
Suggested vegetables:	3 cloves
1 carrot, diced	30–60 ml / 2–4 tbsp lemon juice

1 Fry (sauté) the onions and garlic in a large pan.

2 Add the stock and the remaining ingredients, and simmer until all is cooked.

3 Cooked rice may be added to this soup if liked.

LABAN SOUPPA
Cold Yoghurt Soup

*Y*oghurt may seem an unusual base for a soup, but this is a refreshing dish for a hot summer's day.

◆§ SERVES 6 §◆

3 cucumbers	5 ml / 1 tsp dried dill (dill weed)
1.5 ml / ½ tsp salt	600 ml / 1 pt / 2½ cups natural (plain) yoghurt
2 garlic cloves	
15 ml / 1 tbsp vinegar	GARNISH
1 onion, very finely chopped (optional)	15 ml / 1 tbsp chopped mint

1   Peel the cucumbers, quarter them lengthways and cut into slices 5 mm/¼ in thick. Place in a bowl and sprinkle with salt.

2   Rub another bowl with the garlic and swirl the vinegar around to give flavour, or preferably mash the garlic into the vinegar.

3   The onion, if used, must be put in at this stage.

4   Add the dill and yoghurt, and whisk until the mixture is thick.

5   Pour over the cucumber, stir well and refrigerate. Serve garnished with chopped mint.

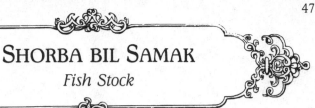

SHORBA BIL SAMAK
Fish Stock

*T*he fish from the areas of the Red Sea and the Arabian Gulf are
generally firmly fleshed which makes them ideal for a soup. It
is often coloured with saffron threads or thickened with egg yolks. It
may be flavoured with lemon juice, vinegar, mint or spices such as
cinnamon or cumin.

MAKES ABOUT 2 1/3 ½ pts / 8 ½ cups

1 kg / 2 lb fish bones and heads	1 carrot, quartered
2 onions, quartered	2.25 l/ 4 pts / 10 cups water

1 Place all the ingredients in a pan. Bring slowly to the boil, removing
   the scum as it rises.

2 Simmer slowly for 20 minutes and strain. Do not cook a fish stock
   for longer as it is not necessary.

SAMAK SOUPPA
Fish Soup

*Y*ou can use any firm white fish (cod, haddock, rock-salmon, etc.)
for this cinnamon-dusted soup. Make the stock according to the
recipe on page 47.

◄§ SERVES 6 §►

1.2 l / 2 pts / 5 cups good fish stock	1 egg yolk beaten with a little cold stock or water
1 onion, chopped	30 ml / 2 tbsp chopped parsley or fennel
1 garlic clove, crushed	
450 g / 1 lb firm white fish, cubed	Cinnamon

1 Put the stock, onion and garlic into a pan and bring slowly to the boil. Add the pieces of fish and simmer until the fish is cooked – about 8–10 minutes.

2 Remove the pan from the heat and slowly pour in the egg yolk mixture, stirring carefully. Return the pan to the heat, but do not let it boil or the egg will curdle.

3 When hot, serve with a sprinkling of fennel or parsley and a dusting of cinnamon.

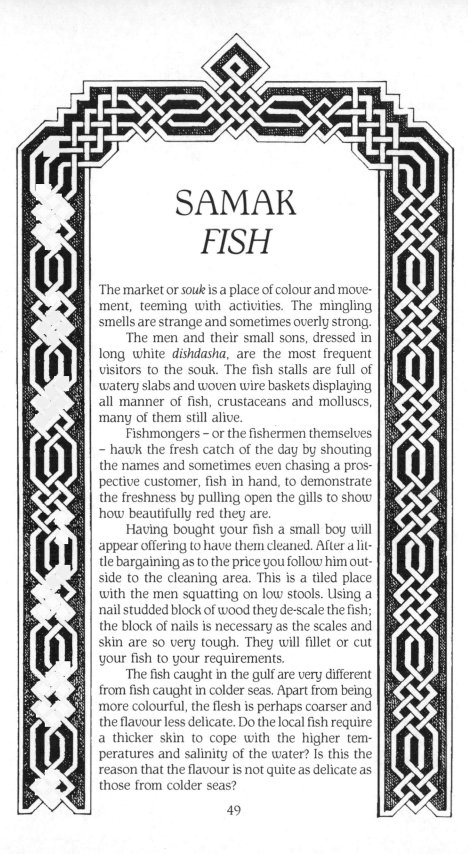

SAMAK
FISH

The market or *souk* is a place of colour and movement, teeming with activities. The mingling smells are strange and sometimes overly strong.

The men and their small sons, dressed in long white *dishdasha*, are the most frequent visitors to the souk. The fish stalls are full of watery slabs and woven wire baskets displaying all manner of fish, crustaceans and molluscs, many of them still alive.

Fishmongers – or the fishermen themselves – hawk the fresh catch of the day by shouting the names and sometimes even chasing a prospective customer, fish in hand, to demonstrate the freshness by pulling open the gills to show how beautifully red they are.

Having bought your fish a small boy will appear offering to have them cleaned. After a little bargaining as to the price you follow him outside to the cleaning area. This is a tiled place with the men squatting on low stools. Using a nail studded block of wood they de-scale the fish; the block of nails is necessary as the scales and skin are so very tough. They will fillet or cut your fish to your requirements.

The fish caught in the gulf are very different from fish caught in colder seas. Apart from being more colourful, the flesh is perhaps coarser and the flavour less delicate. Do the local fish require a thicker skin to cope with the higher temperatures and salinity of the water? Is this the reason that the flavour is not quite as delicate as those from colder seas?

49

There are many varieties which can be cooked in numerous ways and they are all good to eat. Often one type of fish will be substituted for another, depending on the catch of the day.

When buying, choose fish that have clear eyes, bright red gills and whose flesh is firm and glistening; fresh fish should have no smell except, perhaps, that of the sea. Unless you plan to freeze some, buy only enough for your immediate needs.

COUSBAREIAH SAUCE
Rich Fish Sauce

A wonderful sauce made with nuts, this makes a perfect
accompaniment to fish dishes. It adds zest to fried or charcoal
grilled fish.

◄§ S E R V E S 6 §►

30 ml / 2 tbsp oil	2.5 ml / ½ tsp allspice
1 onion, thinly sliced	5 ml / 1 tsp salt
2 tomatoes, sliced	2.5 ml / ½ tsp pepper
50 g / 2 oz / ½ cup almonds, chopped	30 ml / 2 tbsp chopped parsley
50 g / 2 oz / ½ cup walnuts, chopped	15 ml / 1 tbsp finely chopped coriander (cilantro)
50 g / 2 oz / ½ cup pine nuts	

Plain rice and salad to serve

1 Heat the oil and fry (sauté) the onion until golden brown.

2 Add the tomatoes and the nuts and fry for 2–3 minutes, stirring
constantly.

3 Add 50 ml/2 fl oz/3½ tbsp water, the allspice, salt, pepper, parsley
and coriander. Continue to cook for 5 more minutes. This sauce can
be used to pour over the cooked fish or the fish may be cooked in
the sauce in a pre-heated oven for about 20 minutes. Serve with
plain rice and salad.

SAMAK FI AS SINIYAH
Baked Fish with Vegetables

*T*ry anything from sea trout to monkfish tail for this delicious
dish. The fish may either be baked, or cooked on top of the
stove with vegetables and spices. It is served with plain rice and
fried pine nuts.

◆§ S E R V E S 4 - 6 §◆

About 1.5 kg / 3 lb whole fish	1 lemon, peeled and sliced
Pinch of cumin	4–6 potatoes, sliced
Salt and pepper	7.5 ml / 1½ tsp chopped coriander (cilantro)
2 onions, sliced	
3 tomatoes, sliced	30 ml / 2 tbsp fried pine nuts

1   Skin and fillet the fish, but leave in one piece if you can.

2   Pat the fish dry with kitchen paper and sprinkle it on all sides with a
     little cumin, salt and pepper.

3   Grease a deep baking dish (pan) and lay the fish in the centre.

4   Place the onion and tomato slices on top of the fish, then the lemon
     slices and finally the potato slices over all.

5   Cover and bake in the oven at 180°C/350°F/gas mark 4 for 20–30
     minutes.

6   To serve, place the fish very carefully on to a serving plate with the
     vegetables on top. Sprinkle with coriander. Surround it with plain
     rice sprinkled with the fried pine nuts.

SAMAK QUWARMAH
Fish Curry

*Y*ou can adjust the strength of the curry to suit your own taste.
Do not overcook or the fish will fall apart. Use whatever fish is
available.

◆§ SERVES 4 – 6 §◆

675 g / 1½ lb fish steaks or fillets	5 ml / 1 tsp baharat (page 14)
Salt	2.5 ml / ½ tsp turmeric
30 ml / 2 tbsp oil	1 small piece of cinnamon stick
2 onions, chopped	2 loomi (dried limes) or thinly peeled rind of half a lemon or lime
5 ml / 1 tsp grated root ginger (gingerroot)	100 g / 4 oz / 1 cup chopped peeled tomatoes
2 garlic cloves, crushed	120 ml / 4 fl oz / ½ cup water
2.5 ml / ½ tsp hot chilli powder	Plain rice to serve

1 Wash and wipe the fish then cut into serving pieces, sprinkle with
salt, cover and leave aside in a cool place.

2 Heat the oil in a heavy pan, add the onion and fry (sauté) gently
until transparent. Add the ginger, garlic, chilli, baharat, turmeric and
cinnamon stick, and stir over heat for 2 minutes.

3 Add the loomi pierced twice with a skewer, the tomatoes, water and
salt to taste, bring to a slow simmer, cover and simmer gently for 15
minutes.

4 Place the pieces of fish in the sauce, cover and simmer for 15
minutes more until the fish is cooked through.

5 To serve, place the fish on a serving plate, remove the loomi and
cinnamon stick and pour over the sauce. Serve with plain rice.

SAMAK BITAWABIL
Spiced Fish

C *areful presentation of the simply cooked fish makes this dish
appealing to the eye as well as the palate. Use any white fish,
such as bass, small cod or pollack.*

◆§ S E R V E S 6 §◆

1 whole white fish, about 1 kg / 2 lb	½ bunch coriander (cilantro), chopped
1.5 ml / ¼ tsp baharat (page 14)	Salt and pepper
Salt and pepper	300 ml / ½ pt / 1¼ cups tahini
15 ml / 1 tbsp oil	450 ml / ¾ pt / 2 cups water
SAUCE	150 ml / ¼ pt / ⅔ cup lemon juice
15 ml / 1 tbsp oil	GARNISH
1 onion, chopped	15 ml / 1 tbsp olive oil
30 ml / 2 tbsp pine nuts	

1   Sprinkle the cleaned fish with baharat, salt and pepper, then sprinkle
over 15 ml/1 tbsp of oil.

2   Cook the fish in the oven at 180°C/350°F/gas mark 4 for about 20
minutes until tender. Carefully remove all skin and bones, but do not
disturb the shape if possible.

3   Meanwhile make the sauce. Heat the oil then fry (sauté) the onion
until soft, add the coriander, salt and pepper.

4   Put the tahini into a bowl then gradually add the water and lemon
juice, mixing all the time until the ingredients are fully blended.

5   Pour the sauce over the onion mixture, mix well and cook for 2 minutes.

6   For the garnish, heat the oil and fry the pine nuts until golden.

7   To serve, place the cooked fish on to a serving plate, moulding it to
its fish shape. The head can be kept to complete the shape if liked.
Cover with the sauce and garnish with the pine nuts. Serve hot or cold.

SAMAK KAMOUNIEH
Baked Fish with Cumin

*T*his recipe comes from Egypt where it is considered a simple and wholesome meal that is traditionally served with plain rice. Alternative vegetables are sometimes used when making the sauce, such as celery or leeks.

◆§ SERVES 4 – 6 §◆

60 ml /4 tbsp oil	5 ml / 1 tsp salt
3 onions, thinly sliced	1.5 ml / ¼ tsp pepper
2 garlic cloves, crushed	300 ml / ½ pt / 1¼ cups water
5 ml / 1 tsp cumin	1 kg / 2 lb cod or other fish steaks
30 ml / 2 tbsp tomato purée (paste)	3 tomatoes, thinly sliced

1   Heat half the oil in a pan then add the onion, garlic and cumin, and fry (sauté) until golden brown.

2   Stir in the tomato purée, half the salt, the pepper and the water and cook until most of the water has evaporated and the mixture has thickened.

3   Wash and dry the fish then arrange in a greased shallow ovenproof dish.

4   Sprinkle the remaining salt, then the tomato based sauce over the fish.

5   Arrange the tomato slices over the top and sprinkle on the remaining oil.

6   Cover the fish with a lid or foil and cook in the oven at 180°C/350°F/ gas mark 4 for about 20 minutes. Check the liquid and if necessary add a little more.

7   Remove the cover and cook for a further 20 minutes so that the tomatoes can lightly brown.

SAMKE HARRAH AL SAHARA
Baked Fish with Hot Chilli Sauce

*T*his delicious recipe originally comes from the Lebanon, where it is very popular.

◄§ SERVES 6-8 §►

1.75 kg /4 lb red mullet or snapper	150 ml / ¼ pt / ⅔ cup water
Salt	150 ml / ¼ pt / ⅔ cup lemon juice
150 ml / ¼ pt / ⅔ cup oil	1.5 ml / ¼ tsp chilli powder
4–6 garlic cloves	GARNISH
½ bunch coriander (cilantro), finely chopped	15 ml / 1 tbsp pine nuts
300 ml / ½ pt / ⅔ cup tahini	Lemon wedges
	Sprigs of coriander (cilantro)

1 Clean and skin the fish but leave the head on. Wipe dry with kitchen paper then slash the body in 2 places on both sides. Sprinkle with salt and refrigerate for 1–2 hours.

2 Heat all but 15 ml/1 tbsp of the oil in large frying pan (skillet) and fry (sauté) the fish on high heat for a few minutes each side but do not cook through. Carefully lift out of the pan and place in a baking dish.

3 Crush the garlic with 5 ml/1 tsp salt then mix in the finely chopped coriander.

4 Remove most of the oil from the frying pan and fry the garlic mixture until crisp but do not burn. Leave to cool.

5 Place the tahini in a bowl and beat well, then gradually add the water, beating constantly. The mixture will thicken. Beat in the lemon juice and garlic mixture, chilli pepper and salt to taste. If the mixture is too thick add a little more water or lemon juice.

6   Pour the sauce over the fish in the baking dish, covering it completely. Bake in a moderate oven at 180°C/350°F/gas mark 4 for 30 minutes or until the fish is cooked through and the sauce bubbling.

7   While the fish is cooking, fry the pine nuts in a little oil until brown, taking care as they burn easily.

8   To serve, remove the fish from the pan, place on to a serving dish and spoon the sauce over the top. Sprinkle with pine nuts and garnish with the lemon wedges and sprigs of coriander. Serve hot.

SAMAK MAALI
Fried Fish

S ardines or red mullet are popular cooked in this way but any small whole fish, even lemon sole or plaice, can be used. It is also suitable for tiny fish like whitebait, sprats or anchovies.

    If the fish to be fried has a very coarse skin, there is no need to coat in flour or a batter as the skin itself will protect the delicate flesh of the fish. The skin is not usually eaten.

SERVES 4 – 6

1 kg / 2 lb small whole fish, washed and cleaned	Salt and pepper
Plain (all-purpose) flour for coating	Oil for frying

1   Coat the fish with flour seasoned with salt and pepper, and fry (sauté) in hot oil a few pieces at a time. Drain on kitchen paper.

2   Serve with a salad and lemon wedges.

SAMAK HARRAH
Fish Stuffed with Walnuts and Pomegranate Seeds

*T*his is a festive dish for a special occasion. It is probably of
Turkish origin as most Arabic fish recipes are much simpler. It
is an extremely attractive dish with the red of the pomegranate
seeds contrasting with the black olives and green pistachio nuts,
creating a most colourful effect.

SERVES 8

1.5–1.75 kg / 3–4 lb whole sea bass or bream	15 ml / 1 tbsp pomegranate seeds
10 ml / 2 tsp salt	GARNISH
A little oil	Lettuce leaves
1 onion, finely chopped	8–10 black olives
1 green (bell) pepper, chopped	15 ml / 1 tbsp chopped parsley
45 ml / 3 tbsp chopped walnuts	5 ml / 1 tsp pine nuts, lightly fried
60 ml / 4 tbsp chopped parsley	15 ml / 1 tbsp pomegranate seeds
	Lemon slices

1 Clean and scale the fish leaving the head and tail intact. Sprinkle the
   inside and out with salt and a little oil. Leave to stand.

2 To make the stuffing, lightly fry (sauté) the onions until lightly
   brown, add the green pepper and the walnuts, frying for a further
   5 minutes. Add the parsley and pomegranate seeds.

3 Fill the fish with the stuffing, securing the opening with thread or
   skewers.

4 Place the fish in a baking tin in the oven and bake at 180°C/350°F/
   gas mark 4 for about 45 minutes, basting occasionally with its own
   juices.

5 Serve on a bed of chopped lettuce leaves, garnished with the olives
   and parsley. Sprinkle with the pine nuts and the remaining
   pomegranate seeds. Place the lemon slices around the dish.

SAMAK BIL TARATOUR
Fish with Tahini

T *his fish recipe is particularly suitable for special occasions.*
Prepare it in advance, decorate it, then chill until you are
ready to serve.

◄§ SERVES 4 - 6 §►

1 kg / 2 lb whole fish (red mullet, snapper, etc.)	15 ml / 1 tbsp finely chopped coriander (cilantro)
A little oil	Salt and pepper
About 60 ml / 4 tbsp water	GARNISH
Juice of 2 lemons	Pomegranate seeds
150 ml / ¼ pt / ⅔ cup tahini	30 ml / 2 tbsp pine nuts, lightly fried
2 garlic cloves, crushed	1 black olive
Lemon slices	

1   Clean and scale the fish, leaving on the head and tail. Rub it with a
little oil. Place in a baking tin and bake for 20 minutes at 180°C/
350°F/gas mark 4.

2   Cool the fish sufficiently to remove the skin and bones very
carefully, as you want to retain the shape of the fish.

3   Gradually add the water and lemon juice alternately to the tahini
until a thick sauce forms. Stir in the crushed garlic and coriander
and season with salt and pepper to taste.

4   Coat the body of the fish with the sauce and smooth with a spatula,
leaving the head and tail uncovered. Arrange the pomegranate seeds
and lightly fried pine nuts decoratively down the body of the fish.
Replace the eye with an olive, and arrange the lemon slices and
coriander around the fish.

5   Chill well before serving.

KIBBEH SAMAK
Fish Kibbe

B *urghul makes a simple and delicious accompaniment to cod or
other white fish. Pre-cooked burghul is now available in
packets, and only needs a light soaking in hot water to swell the
grains.*

◦§ SERVES 4-6 §◦

450 g / 1 lb / 4 cups fine burghul
wheat

1 kg / 2 lb cod or other white fish
fillets

1 large onion, finely chopped

60 ml / 4 tbsp finely chopped
coriander (cilantro)

15 ml / 1 tbsp chopped parsley

Grated rind of 1 orange

Salt and pepper

FILLING

60 ml / 4 tbsp olive oil

60 ml / 4 tbsp pine nuts

2 large onions, sliced

1   Put the burghul into a large bowl and just cover with boiling water,
    then leave to stand for 15 minutes.

2   Remove any skin and bones from the fish and chop the flesh
    roughly. Put the fish and chopped onion into a food processor and
    process until fine.

3   Combine the fish mixture with the burghul, coriander, parsley,
    orange rind, salt and pepper to taste. Knead to a firm paste. It may
    be necessary to do the processing in small amounts.

4   Heat the oil and brown the pine nuts, remove them, then add the
    sliced onion and fry until transparent.

5   Grease a baking dish (pan) with a little oil and spread half the fish
    mixture on the base. Put the onion and pine nut mixture on top then
    the remaining fish mixture, spread evenly with a spatula to keep the
    filling in place. Cut through in diamond shapes with a sharp knife,
    pour over a little oil and bake in the oven at 200°C/400°F/gas mark 6
    for 30–35 minutes until golden brown. Serve hot or cold.

AL MANKOUAT SAMAK
Fish Marinades

O il, spices and lemon juice are used to marinate fish or brushed on when grilling (broiling). The marinade may also be used as a cooking medium for baking the fish. Here are two examples of marinades that will enhance any fish recipe. They are for about 1 kg/2 lb of fish.

MARINADE 1	MARINADE 2
75 ml / 5 tbsp olive oil	1 onion, sliced
5 ml / 1 tsp black pepper	5 ml / 1 tsp salt
30 ml /2 tbsp lemon juice	2.5 ml / ½ tsp pepper
15 ml / 1 tbsp salt	5 ml / 1 tsp ground cumin
2.5 ml / ½ tsp allspice	45 ml / 3 tbsp olive oil
	30 ml / 2 tbsp lemon juice
	1 garlic clove
	4 bay leaves

1 Clean the fish and dry with kitchen paper.

2 Mix the marinade ingredients of your choice in a shallow dish.

3 Add the fish and coat all over with the marinade, then set aside for 2 hours.

4 The fish can then be grilled (broiled) or cooked over charcoal, basting frequently with the marinade. To test, use a fork and if it flakes easily the fish is cooked. Transfer to a large plate and serve immediately.

FESSIH
Dried Fish

*T*oday fish are still sun-dried and then transported to lands far beyond coastal villages. An area of beach may be covered by thousands of drying fish which are then put into sacks and taken to market.

Dried whole anchovies are ground and used as a marinade for grilling or to top thin rounds of bread called ragag. Prawns (shrimp) are also dried to be used later in the off season. Huge planks of young shark and other fish are dried, to be used later in stews.

RIBANNE
Prawns

*T*he Arabian Gulf has an abundance of prawns (shrimp) of all sizes from the very small to king size. When buying they should be a transparent grey, and should not smell.

To prepare the prawns for cooking, remove the shell with a sharp knife and make a slit down the back. The black vein can now be easily removed.

Prawns may be cooked in two ways:

Method 1

The simplest method is to drop the prawns into boiling water, flavoured with spices or garlic etc. The prawns will be cooked when they have turned pink. Do not over cook them or they will be tough.

Method 2

Prepare the prawns as above. Melt some butter and a little oil in a pan, add 1 or 2 crushed garlic cloves and a little salt and pepper. When hot add the prawns and cook for 1–2 minutes, shaking the pan from time to time until they turn pink.

MAHAAR
Clams

*C*lams live in the shallow, sandy areas of the Arabian Gulf and
Red Sea. As they are seasonal they are only available at
certain times of the year. There are two sizes, the smooth shelled
species called cherry clams which are extremely succulent, and the
larger ribbed variety which are rather more meaty.

The basic method for cooking clams is to boil them in water
for 1–2 minutes. The water may be flavoured with herbs and garlic.
When cooked the shells will open, and the clam can then easily be
removed. Any which do not open should be discarded.

SABBAR
Squid

*O*ne squid is usually sufficient for one person, unless it is
unusually small. To clean, remove the outer purple skin, either
by scraping with a sharp knife or simply pulling it off. Remove the
head and pull the contents from the body. Rinse well in running
water.

The simplest way to cook it is to fry (sauté) it. Cut the squid
into 1 cm/½ in rings and cut the tentacles into small pieces. Dip in
flour or batter and fry in butter, adding garlic, fennel or parsley to
the butter if preferred. Serve with slices of lemon.

MAHSHI SABBAR
Stuffed Squid

S quid may be cooked as below with the addition of a little
tomato purée (paste) to the lemon juice for the last simmering.
They may also be left unstuffed and cooked as below.

◆§ SERVES 4 - 6 §◆

1 kg / 2 lb small squid	50 g / 2 oz / ½ cup pine nuts
15 ml / 1 tbsp oil	3–4 saffron threads
2 onions, finely chopped	Salt and pepper
100 g / 4 oz / 2 cups long-grain rice, washed	120 ml / 4 fl oz / ½ cup water
1 garlic clove, crushed	60 ml / 4 tbsp lemon juice
	Arabic bread to serve

1   Clean the squid as in the previous recipe, then wipe dry on kitchen
    paper.

2   To make the stuffing, lightly fry (sauté) the onion in the oil, add the
    rice and fry for a further 2 minutes. Add the tentacles, garlic, pine
    nuts, saffron, salt and pepper and water. Cover and simmer until all
    the liquid has been absorbed.

3   Fill each squid with the stuffing, packing it in loosely as the rice will
    expand. Secure the opening with small skewers or cocktails sticks
    (toothpicks).

4   Gently fry the squid in a little oil then add the lemon juice and a
    little water. Simmer until they are tender.

5   Serve hot with Arabic bread.

MACHBOUS
Spiced Prawns and Rice

T *his is a favourite of many people in the Arabian Gulf countries as it is a simple and tasty dish to prepare. The prawns and rice are cooked together as in a biryani. The spicy prawn rice is often served with a chilli tomato sauce famous in Kuwait called* daqous.

◆§ SERVES 4 - 6 §◆

1 large onion, chopped	5 ml / 1 tsp chopped coriander (cilantro)
45 ml / 3 tbsp oil	
450 g / 1 lb / 2 cups basmati rice, washed	Salt and pepper
	1 l / 1¾ pt / 4¼ cups water
15 ml / 1 tbsp baharat (page 14)	1 kg / 2 lb prawns (shrimp)
1 tomato, peeled and chopped	2 garlic cloves, crushed
2.5 ml / ½ tsp turmeric	Arabic bread and salad to serve

1 Fry (sauté) the onions in 30 ml/2 tbsp of the oil. Add the rice, baharat, tomato, turmeric, coriander, salt, pepper and water. Cover and simmer for 15 minutes.

2 Shell and de-vein the prawns and lightly fry with the garlic in the remaining 15 ml/1 tbsp oil.

3 Add the prawns and garlic to the rice, cover the pan and continue to cook over low heat for about 5 minutes. The liquid should have been absorbed and the rice cooked.

4 Serve with Arabic bread and a salad.

CIGALES
Cigales

*O*f all the fish in the Gulf, Cigales are one of the best. These
brown rectangular crustaceans may be compared in texture
and flavour to a lobster. During the season of October to January
they come to the surface, attracted to the bright lights of the fishing
boats, and are easily scooped up with nets.

Cigales *should be bought when alive as this is the only
way to ensure they are fresh. They are not readily available in
Britain, but Dublin Bay Prawns (Jumbo Shrimp) can be cooked in
the same way.*

*I have tried various methods of cooking these delicious
shellfish and have come to the conclusion that the following simple
methods of cooking are probably the best.*

*Depending on the other food served, two or three per
person should be sufficient.*

Method 1

1 Bring a large pan of water to the boil, add salt and any herbs
available, such as fennel, parsley, bay leaf and/or a little onion.

2 Add a few cigales at a time as the water should not go off the boil.
Lower the heat and lightly boil until cooked. Unless they are very
big 3–4 minutes should be sufficient.

3 To remove the shell, place the cigale on its back. Cut the shell down
both sides or in the centre and prise apart, the flesh can then be
lifted out.

Method 2

1 Reduce the initial cooking time by 1 minute, then remove the flesh
and cut in half down the centre.

2 Melt some butter with a crushed garlic clove and quickly fry (sauté)
the cigales for a minute or two.

With these two methods they may be eaten hot or cold and are delicious
either way. Serve with a twist of lemon.

Method 3

To barbecue the cigales place on the hot fire on their backs with a little
lemon juice added. Cook until the shells are slightly charred. Serve with
butter and lemon wedges.

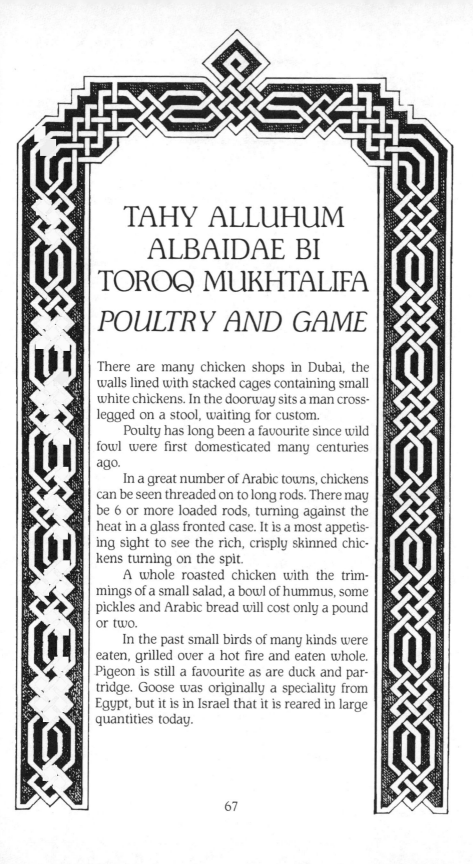

TAHY ALLUHUM ALBAIDAE BI TOROQ MUKHTALIFA

POULTRY AND GAME

There are many chicken shops in Dubai, the walls lined with stacked cages containing small white chickens. In the doorway sits a man cross-legged on a stool, waiting for custom.

Poulty has long been a favourite since wild fowl were first domesticated many centuries ago.

In a great number of Arabic towns, chickens can be seen threaded on to long rods. There may be 6 or more loaded rods, turning against the heat in a glass fronted case. It is a most appetising sight to see the rich, crisply skinned chickens turning on the spit.

A whole roasted chicken with the trimmings of a small salad, a bowl of hummus, some pickles and Arabic bread will cost only a pound or two.

In the past small birds of many kinds were eaten, grilled over a hot fire and eaten whole. Pigeon is still a favourite as are duck and partridge. Goose was originally a speciality from Egypt, but it is in Israel that it is reared in large quantities today.

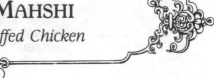

Dajaj Mahshi
Roasted Stuffed Chicken

*A*t many Middle Eastern feasts, a roasted stuffed chicken will be presented along with a whole lamb. The chicken may be filled with a great variety of ingredients from burghul and nuts to vegetables, fruit and rice or chick peas. Many would include whole hard boiled (hard-cooked) eggs, while in Algeria or Morocco couscous and apricots would be used. In the Gulf area a good basmati rice and pine nuts impart an exquisite flavour.

This was originally a Syrian speciality but has long been popular throughout the Middle East. There is an ancient twelfth-century manuscript, 'Kitab al Wusla Ila Habib', which lists over 400 recipes for chicken including this one.

•§ SERVES 6–8 §•

30 ml / 2 tbsp oil	250 ml / 8 fl oz / 1 cup water
1 onion, finely chopped	15 ml / 1 tbsp sultanas (golden raisins)
1 garlic clove, crushed	
1.75 kg / 4 lb whole chicken with the liver and heart	15 ml / 1 tbsp salt
	5 ml / 1 tsp pepper
50 g / 2 oz / ½ cup pine nuts	25 g / 1 oz / 2 tbsp butter
225 g / 8 oz / 1 cup basmati rice, washed	150 ml / ¼ pt / ⅔ cup natural (plain) yoghurt
Mixed salad to serve	

1   Heat the oil in a large pan then add the onion and fry (sauté) until golden brown. Add the garlic.

2   Coarsely chop the chicken liver and heart, and add to the onion with the pine nuts. Fry for 3 minutes, then stir in the rice and continue to cook for a further 2–3 minutes.

3   Add the water, sultanas, 10 ml/2 tsp salt and 2.5 ml/½ tsp pepper and bring to the boil. Reduce the heat and simmer for about 8 minutes or until the water has been absorbed.

4   Remove the pan from the heat and stir in the melted butter.

5   Wash and dry the chicken then spoon the rice mixture into the
    cavity. Secure the opening with a skewer or thread.

6   Mix the yoghurt with the remaining salt and pepper then brush this
    mixture over the chicken.

7   Cook in the oven at 180°C/350°F/gas mark 4 for 1½ hours, basting
    occasionally with the yoghurt mixture. Serve with a mixed salad.

ARNHAB PLAKI
Rabbit with Vegetables

*R*abbit or rabbit joints are now readily available in most
supermarkets. It is a very tasty meat and makes a change from
the usual choices.

◆§ S E R V E S 4 - 6 §◆

100 g / 4 oz / ½ cup butter	275 g / 10 oz carrots
1 rabbit, cut into joints	2 leeks
100 g / 4 oz / 1 cup onions, chopped	1 kg / 2 lb / 8 cups ripe tomatoes, chopped
30 ml / 2 tbsp chopped garlic	
450 g / 1 lb potatoes	Salt and pepper
	Chicken stock

1   Heat the butter in a frying pan and fry the rabbit until brown all
    over. Put into a casserole (Dutch oven).

2   Fry (sauté) the onions until just golden, add the garlic and the
    remaining vegetables. Fry for 2 minutes then add to the casserole.
    Add the chopped tomatoes and enough stock to come half way up
    the rabbit. Simmer for approximately one hour or until the rabbit is
    tender and the sauce has thickened.

3   Place the rabbit in the centre of a large plate and arrange the
    vegetables around the edge.

QUWARMAH ALA DAJAJ
Curried Chicken

*T*he Middle East has always been a great meeting place for the
exchange of cultures, whether in ideas, food or the many
methods of cooking. So it is with the Indian spices, which have
followed the 'Spice Trail' over hundreds of years, each country
adding a little or maybe altering a spice or two, depending on what
is available. It is the Arabic spice mixture baharat (see page 14)
that has replaced the Indian garam masala, though it is very
similar. Using the same spices the proportions are different. Like
garam masala, each family will have its own special mixture.
     Loomis are whole or ground dried limes used to give a
sour flavour to savoury dishes.

SERVES 6

1.5 kg / 3 lb chicken pieces	1.5 ml / ¼ tsp chilli powder
7.5 ml / 1½ tsp baharat (page 14)	Salt and pepper
2.5 ml / ½ tsp turmeric	1 piece cinnamon stick
30 ml / 2 tbsp oil	4 large tomatoes, peeled and chopped
2 large onions, chopped	
2 garlic cloves, crushed	2 loomis, pierced twice or 1 fresh lime, quartered
5 ml / 1 tsp grated root ginger (gingerroot)	

1 Wash the chicken pieces and wipe dry.

2 Combine the baharat with the turmeric then rub half all over the
chicken, leave for half an hour.

3 Heat the oil in a heavy pan and brown the chicken pieces all over,
remove and set aside.

4 Fry the onion until transparent, then add the remaining spice
mixture plus the garlic, ginger, chilli, salt, pepper and cinnamon
stick; fry for 5 more minutes, stirring often.

5   Add the tomatoes, loomis or lime quarters, water and salt to taste. Bring to the boil and add the chicken pieces. Reduce the heat, cover the pan and simmer for about 1½ hours until the chicken is tender and the sauce is thick. Remove the cinnamon stick and the loomis or lime quarters, if preferred. Serve hot with rice.

DAJAJ MASHWI BILBAHARAT
Baharat-flavoured Grilled Chicken

I have not given exact quantities for the lemon juice and spice in this recipe, as it is very much a personal choice. Points to remember are that the flavour of the lemon juice and the baharat will become stronger according to the amount used, and the length of time it is left to marinate on the chicken pieces.

SERVES 4-6

4–6 chicken pieces	Salt and pepper
Juice of 1 or 2 lemons	GARNISH
Approx 5-10 ml/1-2 tsp baharat (page 14)	Chopped parsley or coriander (cilantro)
Garlic sauce (page 102)	

1   Remove the skin from the chicken and wipe well. Pour over the lemon juice and leave to stand for 30 minutes or so.

2   Cover each piece of chicken with a sprinkling of baharat and a little salt and pepper.

3   To cook the chicken: the pieces may be placed under a grill (broiler) turning once or twice, or they may be cooked in a frying pan (skillet) with a little oil and a well-fitting lid until tender.

4   Place the chicken pieces on a plate, sprinkle over a little parsley or coriander and serve with the garlic sauce.

Dajaj Souryani
Chicken with Yoghurt

*T*his chicken recipe was an old favourite of the Assyrians of ancient times, and like all good things it has been handed down from mother to daughter. This recipe will, I think, give you a hint of the richness and sophistication of that ancient culture.

◆§ SERVES 6–8 §◆

50 g / 2 oz / ¼ cup butter	5 ml / 1 tsp salt
1.5 kg /3 lb chicken, cut into 8 serving pieces	2.5 ml / ½ tsp pepper
1 onion, finely chopped	30 ml / 2 tbsp ground almonds
1 green (bell) pepper, finely sliced	300 ml / ½ pt / 1¼ cups natural (plain) yoghurt
600 ml / 1 pt / 2½ cups chicken stock	5 ml / 1 tsp ground cumin
30 ml / 2 tbsp sumak (page 12)	5 ml / 1 tsp cayenne pepper

1 Melt the butter in a large pan and fry (sauté) the chicken pieces until they are browned all over, then remove from the pan and keep warm.

2 Put the onion and green pepper in the same pan and fry until the onion is soft. Stir in the stock, sumak, salt and pepper.

3 Return the chicken pieces to the pan, put on a lid and simmer on low heat for about 30 minutes until the chicken is tender.

4 Transfer the cooked chicken to a warmed serving dish.

5 Add enough water to the almonds to make a smooth paste, add this to the juices in the pan and bring back to the boil, stirring all the time.

6 Remove the pan from the heat then add the yoghurt to the sauce, mix in well and reheat gently. Pour the sauce over the chicken, sprinkle with the cumin and cayenne pepper and serve immediately.

TAGINE DEJAJ BIL TAMAR
Chicken with Dates

*T*agine, *a North African word for a stew, is also the name of a cooking utensil; it is a round wide earthenware dish with a sharply conical tight fitting lid. It can be placed on hot charcoal to cook slowly until the liquid has been reduced to a thick and lovely sauce.*

◄§ SERVES 4-6 §►

675 g / 1½ lb boneless chicken pieces

225 g / 8 oz / 2 cups chopped onion

1 garlic clove, crushed

30 ml / 2 tbsp la kama spice mix (page 14)

5 ml / 1 tsp cumin seeds

60 ml / 4 tbsp oil

2-3 bay leaves

12-16 dates, stoned and halved

60 ml / 4 tbsp whole almonds

30 ml / 2 tbsp honey

Aromatic salt to taste (page 13)

1   Cut the chicken into bite size pieces.

2   In a heavy pan fry (sauté) the onion, garlic, la kama and cumin seeds in the oil for 15 minutes.

3   Add 600 ml/1 pt/2½ cups of boiling water and the bay leaves. Simmer uncovered for about 30 minutes until the liquid has reduced by about a third.

4   Add the chicken and cook on low heat for 20 minutes, stirring occasionally, and adding a little more stock if necessary.

5   Add the dates, nuts and honey and continue to simmer for a further 10 minutes. Test for seasoning and add aromatic salt as necessary.

6   To serve, place the meat and sauce in the centre of a serving dish and surround with plain rice, pilaff or couscous.

Couscous
Couscous

*I*t was in a leafy courtyard lit only by candle-light and the stars
above, with the scent of orange trees growing nearby, that we
were served the lovely Moroccan dish of couscous.

Our meal consisted of the main course served in a tagine
*(stew pot), with the meat and fruit placed on the base of the dish
and the couscous piled high on top. Served with this was a full-
bodied red wine. Having thoroughly enjoyed the first course, we
were surprised to be served a second couscous. This was presented
to us on a beautiful silver dish, but this time, it was only the grain
with rays of sugared cinnamon and raisins radiating from the top
of the cone. We were delighted and amazed at the lightness of this
sweet. The meal was completed with little cups of strong black
Arabic coffee and small squares of Turkish Delight.*

◄§ SERVES 6 §►

6 chicken pieces	225 g / 8 oz carrots
450 g / 1 lb boneless lamb, cut into cubes	225 g / 8 oz turnips
450 g / 1 lb onions	225 g / 8 oz courgettes (zucchini)
5 ml / 1 tsp salt	100 g / 4 oz green beans
2.5 ml / ½ tsp pepper	450 g / 1 lb tomatoes
5 ml / 1 tsp paprika	450 g / 1 lb pre-cooked couscous (page 138)

1 Put all the meat into a large pan and just cover with water, bring to
the boil and remove the scum as it rises. Add 2 chopped onions, salt,
pepper and paprika then simmer for about 30 minutes.

2 Wash and peel the carrots and turnips, then cut them and the courgettes into quarters lengthwise. Cut the beans in half, peel and chop the tomatoes, quarter the remaining onions, then add all the vegetables to the meat and cook for a further 20 to 30 minutes. The meat should be tender and the vegetables just cooked. The liquid should by this time have been reduced to a thickened sauce.

3 Put the cooked couscous in a large bowl and sprinkle over 1 litre/ 2 pts/5 cups of boiling, salted water, stir so that the water is evenly absorbed and so that the mixture cools slightly. Rub the grains between your hands to fluff up and remove any lumps. Leave the grain to stand for 10 minutes then add a little oil or melted butter. Place the couscous into a colander that has been lined with muslin to prevent the grain falling through, then stand the colander on top of the steaming pan of meat and vegetables. This is to heat the couscous thoroughly. It does not need further cooking.

4 To serve, turn the couscous out on to a large round plate, make a well in the centre then, with a slotted spoon, lift out the meat and vegetables and place in the well. Serve the sauce separately.

VARIATIONS

- Add 170 g/6 oz half-cooked chick peas at the start, with a good pinch of cayenne pepper and cinnamon.

- An alternative presentation, which can look quite spectacular, is to cover the meat completely with the grain shaped to a cone. The vegetables are then placed in alternate colours over the grain radiating out from the tip of the cone. Garnish with a few toasted almonds.

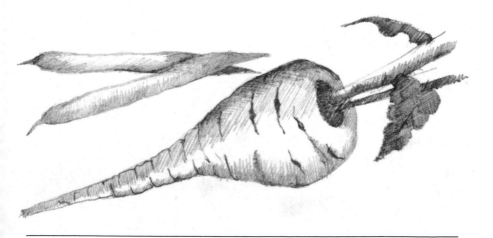

MUSAKHAN
She-has-fever Chicken

*A*s I cannot find a direct answer as to why this dish should be called by such a strange name, I can only surmise that it is the red sumak *that is sprinkled over the chicken and bread just before serving that gives the impression of a fever.*

◄§ SERVES 4 – 6 §►

1 kg / 2 lb chicken pieces	1.5 ml / ¼ tsp cinnamon
Chicken stock	1.5 ml / ¼ tsp nutmeg
Lemon juice	Oil for frying
60 ml / 4 tbsp sumak	5 large onions, quartered
Pepper	60 ml / 4 tbsp pine nuts
Arabic bread	

1   Simmer the chicken in just enough stock to cover until it is almost cooked. Remove the chicken pieces and reserve the stock.

2   Rub the chicken with a little lemon juice, 30 ml/2 tbsp sumak, pepper, cinnamon and nutmeg. Fry (sauté) the pieces until they are brown and tender. Keep warm.

3   Meanwhile, fry (sauté) the onions in a little oil with 15 ml/1 tbsp sumak. Add the pine nuts and fry for a further 2 minutes; add the chicken stock and bring to the boil. Boil rapidly to reduce to a sauce consistency if necessary.

4   To serve, place the chicken pieces on a plate, pour over the sauce and cover with Arabic bread sprinkled with 15 ml/1 tbsp sumak.

FESANJUNE
Duck with Walnuts and Pomegranate

*T*his recipe was served at very special occasions by the Shah of
Persia using a whole peacock. It was presented on a bed of red
pomegranate seeds surrounded by yellow saffron rice. Today we
would use a wild duck or pheasant.

⋈ SERVES 4 – 6 ⋈

1 large oven-ready duck	15 ml / 1 tbsp sugar
1 large onion, chopped	Salt and pepper
225 g / 8 oz walnuts, chopped	GARNISH
75 ml / 5 tbsp grenadine syrup	Pomegranate seeds
30 ml / 2 tbsp lemon juice	Whole walnuts

1   Roast the duck on a grid in a hot oven at 200°C/400°F/gas mark 6
for approximately 1½ hours or until cooked. Remove and break up
into serving pieces. Keep warm. Remove the fat from the pan and put
aside.

2   Fry (sauté) the onions until just coloured then put into the pan in
which the duck was cooked, add the walnuts, grenadine syrup,
lemon juice, sugar and a little water, stir well to incorporate the
juices from the duck. Season well.

3   Cook the sauce until it has thickened, and add more salt if necessary.

4   Place the pieces of duck on a bed of saffron rice with a little of the
sauce poured over; the remainder may be served separately.

5   Garnish with pomegranate seeds and whole walnuts.

HAMAAM MAHSHI
Stuffed Pigeon

*T*his is a very special dish which apart from tasting delicious
looks quite spectacular on a dinner table. Allow one pigeon per
person, but make one or two extra as they are so popular.

⋅§ SERVES 4-6 §⋅

6 pigeons	Pinch of cinnamon
150 g / 5 oz / scant cup butter	2.5 ml / ½ tsp mixed (apple pie) spice
1 small onion, finely chopped	30 ml / 2 tbsp pine nuts
75 g / 3 oz / ⅓ cup minced (ground) beef	15 ml / 1 tbsp chopped parsley
	Oil for frying
100 g / 4 oz / ½ cup long-grain rice	75 g / 3 oz / ¼ cup tomato purée (paste)
Salt and pepper	Salad and Arabic bread to serve

1   Clean and dry the pigeons, sprinkle with salt and set aside.

2   Heat the butter in a pan, fry (sauté) the onion until brown. Add the
    beef and continue to brown, then add the rice and cook for 2
    minutes. Add salt and pepper to taste, the mixed spice, pine nuts and
    parsley, mix well and continue to fry for a further 5 minutes.

3   Add 120 ml/4 fl oz/½ cup of boiling water, lower the heat, and allow
    the water to be absorbed by the rice mixture. The rice is now partly
    cooked. Remove from the heat.

4   Stuff the pigeons with equal quantities of the rice and meat mixture.
    Secure the openings with thread or a skewer. Heat a little oil in a
    deep pan and brown the stuffed pigeons all over, turning frequently
    for about 15–20 minutes.

5   Add 450 ml/1¾ pt/2 cups of boiling water to the tomato purée and
    pour over the pigeons. They should be half covered. Simmer on low
    heat for about 35–40 minutes.

6   To serve, place the pigeons on a serving dish and surround with the
    sauce. Any left over sauce can be served separately. A salad and flat
    Arabic bread should accompany the birds.

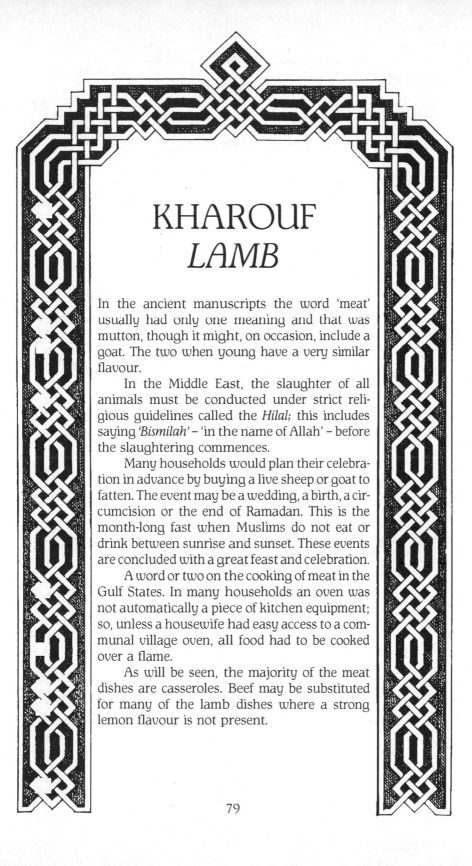

KHAROUF
LAMB

In the ancient manuscripts the word 'meat' usually had only one meaning and that was mutton, though it might, on occasion, include a goat. The two when young have a very similar flavour.

In the Middle East, the slaughter of all animals must be conducted under strict religious guidelines called the *Hilal*; this includes saying *'Bismilah'* – 'in the name of Allah' – before the slaughtering commences.

Many households would plan their celebration in advance by buying a live sheep or goat to fatten. The event may be a wedding, a birth, a circumcision or the end of Ramadan. This is the month-long fast when Muslims do not eat or drink between sunrise and sunset. These events are concluded with a great feast and celebration.

A word or two on the cooking of meat in the Gulf States. In many households an oven was not automatically a piece of kitchen equipment; so, unless a housewife had easy access to a communal village oven, all food had to be cooked over a flame.

As will be seen, the majority of the meat dishes are casseroles. Beef may be substituted for many of the lamb dishes where a strong lemon flavour is not present.

FAKHID KHAROUF BI LABAN
Leg of Lamb Cooked in Yoghurt

F or this recipe a spiced yoghurt is used as a marinade. Not only does it tenderise the meat but it also imparts a very special flavour to a leg of lamb.

◆§ SERVES 8 §◆

2 kg / 4½ lb leg of lamb	2.5 ml / ½ tsp chilli powder
8 garlic cloves	2.5 ml / ½ tsp cinnamon
Salt and pepper	2.5 ml / ½ tsp turmeric or 2–3 threads of saffron (optional)
Olive oil	
600 ml / 1 pt / 2½ cups natural (plain) yoghurt	GARNISH
	Parsley
5 ml / 1 tsp allspice	Lemon wedges

Plain rice to serve

1 Wash and dry the leg of lamb.

2 Make eight small incisions with a pointed knife and insert a whole garlic clove and a minute touch of salt and pepper into each cut.

3 Smear the leg with olive oil.

4 Mix the yoghurt with the spices, saffron (if using) and a little salt and pepper and pour over the meat.

5 Leave the meat to marinate for 2–4 hours in a cool place.

6 Cover and cook in a pre-heated oven, 180°C/350°F/gas mark 4 for 2–2½ hours, basting occasionally with the yoghurt mix.

7 Garnish with parsley and lemon wedges and serve with hot plain rice.

HABEET
Stewed Lamb

*T*he lamb in this recipe, due to the long slow cooking in the loomi-flavoured vinegar and water, becomes so tender as to fall off the bone. The flavour of the meat and the remaining sauce is deliciously aromatic. One of the vegetable casseroles (page 110) or the courgette (zucchini) fritters (page 130) would be a good accompaniment.

◄§ SERVES 4-6 §►

1.5 kg / 3 lb leg of lamb cut into 3 pieces on the bone	150 ml / ¼ pt / ⅔ cup malt or wine vinegar
1 loomi (dried lime) or the thinly peeled rind of ½ lemon or 1 lime	6 garlic cloves, chopped
	Salt and pepper

1 Place the lamb and loomi in a large pan with enough water to just cover. Slowly bring to the boil, removing the scum as it rises.

2 Add the vinegar and garlic.

3 Cover the pan and simmer gently for 2½–3 hours, the liquid should have reduced to a thick sauce and the meat should fall off the bone. Season to taste.

4 Remove the bones and loomi and serve steaming hot.

VARIATION

• Reduce the garlic to 3 cloves and add 2.5 ml/½ tsp turmeric and 15 ml/1 tbsp baharat (page 14).

LABAN UMMO
Lamb Cooked in Yoghurt

*T*his is a most ancient dish that could be said to have come out of the desert. To the Bedouin tribes, water was a most precious commodity and could not always be spared for cooking, whereas milk, which was in almost constant supply from either their goats or camels, was readily available. This is why yoghurt is so often used in Middle Eastern cookery.

SERVES 4 – 6

675 g / 1½ lb lamb, cubed	300 ml / ½ pt / 1¼ cups natural (plain) yoghurt
4 medium onions, chopped	15 ml / 1 tbsp cornflour (cornstarch)
2–4 garlic cloves	GARNISH
5 ml / 1 tsp allspice	Fresh mint or coriander (cilantro)
300 ml / ½ pt / 1¼ cups lamb or chicken stock	Plain rice to serve

1 Place the lamb, onion, garlic, allspice and stock in a casserole (Dutch oven) with a well fitting lid, bake in the oven at 180°C/350°F/gas mark 4 for 40 minutes.

2 Meanwhile stabilise the yoghurt by mixing with the cornflour. Heat this slowly until the sauce thickens, add a little salt.

3 Pour the yoghurt sauce over the lamb and return to the oven. Leave uncovered for a further 15 minutes until the lamb is tender.

4 Garnish with fresh mint or coriander and serve with plain rice.

TAH CHIN
Lamb, Yoghurt and Rice

*I*f you can get the whole 'cake' out in one piece it will look quite
spectacular. If not, spoon the rice and meat mixture on to a
serving dish, lift off the crusty layer from the bottom and break it
into pieces to arrange around the edge of the plate. It can be cut
into wedges like a cake.

◆§ S E R V E S 6 §◆

1 kg / 2 lb lamb, cubed	Salt and pepper
1.2 l / 2 pts / 5 cups natural (plain) yoghurt	2 cups basmati rice
2.5 ml / ½ tsp turmeric or a few threads of saffron	2 egg yolks, beaten
	50 g / 2 oz / ¼ cup butter or oil

1   Combine the lamb with 600 ml/1 pt/2½ cups of the yoghurt, the
    turmeric or saffron threads, and the salt and pepper. Coat the meat
    well all over and leave to marinate overnight.

2   Wash the rice and put into 2 cups of boiling water. Boil uncovered
    for 5 minutes. Remove from the stove and drain well.

3   Beat the egg yolks in a large bowl, then add the remaining yoghurt
    and 350 g/12 oz/1½ cups of the rice.

4   Place the melted butter and 15 ml/1 tbsp hot water in a rectangular
    casserole (Dutch oven) and swirl to coat the sides and base. Spread
    the egg, yoghurt and rice mixture evenly over the base.

5   Arrange half the lamb cubes over this with some of the yoghurt
    marinade. Add a layer of rice, the remaining lamb mixture and all
    but 120 ml/4 fl oz/½ cup of marinade. Then top with the remaining
    rice and spread the reserved yoghurt marinade on top.

6   Cover the casserole with a tight fitting lid or foil and cook in an
    oven at 160°C/325°F/gas mark 3 for 2 hours.

7   Stand the casserole in a bowl of cold water for 5 minutes, run a
    knife around the edge, place a serving dish over the top and turn
    upside down.

MURG BAMIA

Lamb with Okra and Tomatoes

In this recipe the okra and tomatoes combine to give a rich and succulent flavour. The okra also gives the stew a distinctive taste.

◄§ S E R V E S 4 §►

1 large onion, chopped	30 ml / 2 tbsp lemon juice
Oil for frying	15 ml / 1 tbsp sugar
450 g / 1 lb lamb, cubed	Salt and pepper
2 garlic cloves, crushed	Lamb or chicken stock
4 tomatoes, peeled and chopped	225 g / 8 oz fresh okra (ladies' fingers)
30 ml / 2 tbsp tomato purée (paste)	Rice or burghul to serve

1   Brown the onion in a little oil then add the meat, turning the pieces until they are browned all over.

2   Add the garlic, tomatoes, tomato purée, lemon juice, sugar, salt and pepper, and sufficient stock to just cover the meat. Cover the pan and simmer for 30 minutes.

3   Remove the stems from the okra and fry in oil for a minute or two. Add to the stew and simmer for a further 10 minutes.

4   Serve with rice or burghul.

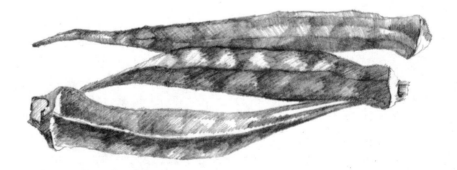

TIMMIM BAGELLA
Lamb with Broad Beans in Rice

S tewed lamb put on to a bed of rice and broad beans is an unusual and interesting combination. If you are using fresh beans, add them to the rice when it is half cooked.

•§ SERVES 4–6 §•

1 kg / 2 lb lamb, cubed	30 ml / 2 tbsp chopped dill (dill weed)
1 large onion, chopped	
5 ml / 1 tsp baharat (page 14)	Salt and pepper
225 g / 8 oz broad (lima) beans, if using dried soak them overnight first	GARNISH
	Chopped parsley
450 g / 1 lb / 2 cups basmati rice	

1   Fry (sauté) the meat, onions and baharat until the meat is brown. Add a little stock and cook gently until the meat is tender.

2   Bring 3 cups of water to the boil, add the beans and boil for 5 minutes. Add the rice and dill, stir gently and cook until the rice and beans are tender. Season with salt and pepper.

3   To serve, spread the rice and beans on to a large serving dish and place the meat on top. Garnish with a little chopped parsley.

DAOUD PASHA
Meatballs and Pine Nuts

*T*his tasty meal is dedicated to Garabed Artin Pasha Davoudian who became the first Governor of Lebanon in 1860. He was a remarkable man who modernised the administration and the economy of the country. He was also considered a connoisseur of good food.

❧ SERVES 4 ☙

450 g / 1 lb minced (ground) lamb	1 onion, thinly sliced
Salt and pepper	60 ml / 4 tbsp pine nuts
2.5 ml / ½ tsp ground cumin	30 ml / 2 tbsp tomato purée (paste) blended with 300 ml / ½ pt / 1¼ cups water
5 ml / 1 tsp ground coriander (cilantro)	
1.5 ml / ¼ tsp allspice	15 ml / 1 tbsp lemon juice
10 button (pearl) onions, peeled	15 ml / 1 tbsp fresh basil, chopped
45 ml / 3 tbsp oil	A little butter for frying

1   In a large bowl mix together the meat, salt, pepper, cumin, 2.5 ml/ ½ tsp coriander and the allspice. Shape the mixture into small balls. Use a little flour if necessary.

2   Heat the oil in a large frying pan (skillet) and lightly fry all the onions until lightly coloured. Add the meatballs and fry for about 10 minutes, stirring occasionally until browned all over.

3   Add half the nuts and fry for a further 2 minutes. Pour in the tomato purée mixture, the remaining coriander, the lemon juice and basil. Stir well, reduce the heat and simmer for about 30 minutes, stirring occasionally until the meat is cooked and the sauce has thickened.

4   Turn the meatballs into a warmed serving dish and keep hot.

5   Melt a little butter in a small frying pan and fry the remaining pine nuts until golden. Stick one nut into each meatball and serve at once with plain rice.

MAKLUBA
Lamb Upside-down

*T*his is another cake-like recipe, easy to prepare but tricky to remove from the cooking vessel in one piece; nevertheless it is a delicious and most attractive dish. Potatoes can be used instead of aubergines as a variation.

SERVES 4 - 6

4 medium aubergines (eggplants), sliced	450 g / 1 lb / 2 cups basmati rice, washed
Oil for frying	150 ml / ¼ pt tomato sauce (page 120)
450 g / 1 lb lamb, cubed	5 ml / 1 tsp cinnamon
2 large onions, chopped	2.5 ml / ½ tsp nutmeg
450 g / 1 lb tomatoes, sliced	2.5 ml / ½ tsp cloves, ground
Salt and pepper	

1 Fry (sauté) the aubergines in oil until lightly browned on both sides.

2 Fry the meat and the onions.

3 Place one layer of aubergines over the base of a large casserole (Dutch oven), a layer of tomatoes, meat and then the uncooked rice. Continue with the layers until all the ingredients are used.

4 To make the sauce, add enough water to the tomato sauce to make up to 600 ml/1 pt/2½ cups, add the spices and bring to the boil. Pour this over the layers; there should be enough to just cover.

5 Cook slowly for 30–45 minutes until the meat is tender and the rice is cooked. The liquid should have been absorbed.

6 To serve, stand the casserole on a cold surface or in cold water for 5 minutes, run a knife around the inside edge, place a serving plate on top of the contents and turn upside-down. Remove the casserole dish. Serve cut into wedges.

MACHBOUS
Spiced Lamb with Rice

*M**achbous is a richly spiced dish using lamb, chicken or fish (see page 65) as the main ingredient; the rice is added to the pot to cook with the meat. The spices may be ground or used whole and removed before serving.*

⋅§ SERVES 4 – 6 §⋅

2 large onions, chopped	3 whole cloves or 5 ml / 1 tsp ground
1 kg / 2 lb lamb pieces	5 ml / 1 tsp cinnamon
4 tomatoes, peeled and chopped	5 ml / 1 tsp turmeric
30 ml / 2 tbsp chopped parsley	750 ml / 1¼ pt / 3 cups stock
15 ml / 1 tbsp baharat (page 14)	Salt and pepper
2 loomi pierced twice or 1 sliced fresh lime or lemon	450 g / 1 lb / 2 cups basmati rice, washed
3 ground cardamom pods (optional)	Salad and Arabic bread to serve

1   Fry the onions until they are brown then add the meat to brown all over.

2   Add the remaining ingredients except the rice and simmer for 30 minutes.

3   Stir the rice into the boiling stock, cover and simmer over a low heat for a further 20 minutes or until the rice is cooked. Fluff with a fork.

4   Serve with a salad and Arabic bread.

MISHMISHIYA
Lamb and Apricots

S trictly speaking the lamb in this recipe should be cut into cubes to stew in a stock. As a variation I thought I would try cooking it in one piece in the oven. It was so good that I have changed the recipe to baking rather than stewing. But if you should prefer a truly authentic dish then the meat should be stewed.

◦§ SERVES 4 - 6 §◦

1 shoulder or leg of lamb	1.5 ml / ¼ tsp ground cumin
A little oil	2.5 ml / ½ tsp ground coriander (cilantro)
4 small onions, peeled	
225 g / 8 oz dried apricots, soaked overnight and drained (or use ready-to-eat ones)	1.5 ml / ¼ tsp cinnamon
	4 saffron threads
30 ml / 2 tbsp almonds	Salt and pepper
1.5 ml / ¼ tsp root ginger (gingerroot), grated	Plain rice and salad to serve

1   Weigh the joint, then roast in the oven at 190°C/375°F/gas mark 5, with a little oil and the peeled onions, allowing 25 minutes per 450 g/1 lb plus 25 minutes over, until three-quarters cooked.

2   Simmer the apricots in a little water until they have swelled. Add the remaining ingredients and blend to a rather coarse purée (paste).

3   Pour the sauce over the meat and return to the oven to complete the cooking, basting from time to time with it own juices.

4   Serve hot with plain rice and a salad.

MANSEF
Lamb with a Yoghurt Sauce

*M*ansef literally translated means 'the large tray' on which the food is served. This is a communal meal for the whole family. Arabic families will often include uncles, aunts and cousins so a whole lamb would be needed, especially as they are considerably smaller than Western sheep. The meat would usually be served resting on a bed of rice on a large tray. Arabic bread would be draped over the meat and used to break off pieces of meat and to scoop up the rice and sauce.

◄§ SERVES 6-8 §►

1 whole shoulder or leg of lamb	A little oil
2 onions, chopped	15 ml / 1 tbsp cornflour (cornstarch)
5 ml / 1 tsp baharat (page 14)	
2-4 garlic cloves, crushed	300 ml / ½ pt / 1¼ cups natural (plain) yoghurt
Salt and pepper	

1   Place the meat with the onions, baharat, garlic and a little oil in a lidded casserole (Dutch oven). Cook in the oven at 190°C/375°F/gas mark 5 for 20 minutes. Turn the meat and return to the oven for a further 20 minutes.

2   Meanwhile mix the cornflour with a little of the yoghurt, add the remaining ingredients and put into a pan to cook slowly, stirring all the time until it thickens. A little milk may be added if it is too thick; add salt and pepper to taste.

3   When the meat has cooked for 40 minutes remove from the oven to cover with the yoghurt sauce, mixed with the juices already in the casserole. Return to the oven uncovered, and cook until the meat is tender (about 1 hour).

MESHWI
OUTDOOR COOKING

During the spring and winter months when the sun is not quite so hot it is a pleasant sight to see Arabs in large numbers enjoying a picnic. It may be on a beach, a stark desert dune or perhaps a *wadi* – a dried-up river bed among the purple mountains. There may even be a stream for the children to paddle in if they are lucky.

The barbecue (grill) will be built close by, for *meshwi*, the art of cooking over the heat of dying embers, is the highlight of any weekend outing. People may even have their tents and carpets with them.

The techniques for barbecuing are varied, with the utensils being designed for each type of food. Pencil-sized skewers are used to thread kebabs, bite-size morsels of meat, fish or vegetables. Spicy minced meat is squeezed into oblong shapes around the foot of long metal spikes, which distribute the heat and prevent the food from falling into the embers.

For all grilled dishes, select the best cuts of meat, removing any tendons or gristle. A little fat may be left on as this prevents the meat drying out. A marinade is used for most meats as this ensures tenderness.

To accompany the grilled meats and fish an assortment of salads and pickles, various breads, dates and cheeses and plenty of fruit would all be there, and to drink there would be fresh bottled spring water.

SAMAK KABAB
Barbecued Seafood

*W*hole grilled fish and large prawns (shrimp) are especially popular in the coastal villages as they are so abundant. Generally Arabs clean the fish but leave on the head. The coarse skin acts as a protective coat for the juicy inner flesh. It is then removed before being eaten.

Any firm-fleshed fish may be barbecued and it can be marinated if wished. For prawns the heads and tails are left on and peeled just before eating.

For small varieties a long skewer can be used. Push the skewer through the fish from head to tail and place over the barbecue, brush lightly with a little oil and turn occasionally.

Here is a recipe for barbecued squid, but it may be applied to any variety of fish.

◄§ SERVES 4-6 §►

1 squid per person	Salt and pepper
3-4 onions, quartered	GARNISH
1 green (bell) pepper, cubed	Lemon wedges and parsley sprigs

1   Clean the squid by removing the purple skin, using a sharp knife or it may be peeled off. Remove the head and pull the contents from the body, rinse well.

2   Cut the squid into 1 cm/½ in rings. Marinate for 1 hour if wished in the marinade of your choice: see page 105.

3   Thread the squid and vegetables alternately on to the skewers. Season with salt and pepper.

4   Grill over the barbecue for about 6-8 minutes or until tender, basting with a marinade, oil or a little lemon juice.

5   Garnish with lemon wedges and parsley.

SHISH TAOUK
Skewered Grilled Chicken

*T*his is one of the simplest ways to barbecue chicken but it is
nevertheless very tasty. Serve with salad and Arabic bread.

SERVES 4 - 6

1 kg / 2 lb boneless chicken	Salt and pepper
150 ml / ¼ pt / ⅔ cup lemon juice	60 ml / 4 tbsp oil or butter
1 large onion, grated	5 ml / 1 tsp paprika

1 Cut the chicken into small cubes, discarding the skin.

2 Combine the lemon juice, onion, salt and pepper; add the chicken
pieces turning in the marinade. Leave to marinate for 3-4 hours in
the refrigerator, turning the pieces occasionally.

3 Thread the chicken cubes on to 6 long flat skewers, placing them
close together and with the thicker pieces in the centre of the
skewers.

4 Combine the oil or butter with the paprika and brush over the
chicken. Cook over glowing charcoal or grill (broil) under a high
heat, reducing to medium. Baste and turn frequently during cooking.

5 Cook for 12-15 minutes, concentrating the heat on the thicker centre
pieces.

6 When cooked the chicken can be removed from the skewers if
preferred.

DAJAJ KABAB
Chicken Kebab

C hicken can be transformed by marinating in this mixture of
*lemon juice and spices. Remove the meat from the skewers
before serving if you prefer.*

◄§ SERVES 4-6 §►

1.5 kg / 3 lb chicken	5 ml / 1 tsp tomato purée (paste)
1 garlic clove, crushed	15 ml / 1 tbsp lemon juice
60 ml / 4 tbsp oil	1.5 ml / ¼ tsp ground cumin
2.5 ml / ½ tsp cayenne pepper	2.5 ml / ½ tsp salt
1.5 ml / ¼ tsp pepper	

1 Wash, dry and skin the chicken and remove all bones. Cut into
   2.5 cm/1 in cubes. Mix all the remaining ingredients together then
   add the chicken pieces. Stir well, making sure all the meat is well
   covered with the spices. Leave for at least 2 hours.

2 Thread on to skewers and grill over charcoal, turning frequently.

SHISH KEBAB
Grilled Lamb Kebab

*T*his is probably the most familiar of all the barbecue grills. It may be varied enormously, using lamb, beef or chicken, mushrooms and other vegetables may be added, and it can be served with a wide variety of sauces.

SERVES 4 - 6

450 g / 1 lb meat, cubed	4 garlic cloves
2 onions, quartered	4 chillies
½ red (bell) pepper, cubed	Arabic bread and lemon wedges to serve
½ green (bell) pepper, cubed	

1 If the meat is at all tough choose a marinade (page 105) to soak the meat in overnight.

2 Thread the meat and vegetables alternately on to skewers. A clove of garlic and a chilli may be added to each skewer.

3 Grill (broil) over the hot barbecue for 8-10 minutes, basting with the marinade or a little oil and turning occasionally.

4 Serve with Arabic bread and lemon wedges.

SHASHLIK KEBAB
Marinated Lamb Kebabs

*T*hese kebabs are ideal if you are entertaining because they need to be prepared a day in advance. They are well worth the effort of preparing the marinade.

◆§ SERVES 6 §◆

25 ml / 1½ tbsp oil	10 ml / 2 tsp brown sugar
200 g / 7 oz / 1 scant cup onions, finely chopped	15 ml / 1 tbsp apricot jam (conserve)
2.5 ml / ½ tsp ground coriander (cilantro)	Salt and pepper
2.5 ml / ½ tsp turmeric	1 kg / 2 lb boneless lamb, cut into 2.5 cm/1 in cubes
2.5 ml / ½ tsp baharat (page 14)	1 garlic clove, crushed
60 ml / 4 tbsp lime juice mixed with 60 ml / 4 tbsp water	12 button (pearl) onions, peeled
	Arabic bread and salad to serve

The day before the barbecue:

1 Heat the oil and gently fry the chopped onions until they are soft and transparent.

2 Add the coriander, turmeric and baharat. Stir for 2-3 minutes.

3 Add the lime juice, water, brown sugar and apricot jam and bring to the boil.

4 Reduce the heat and simmer for 15 minutes. Remove from the heat and allow to cool.

5 Season the lamb cubes. Add the garlic and lamb to the mixture and marinate overnight, turning the meat occasionally.

When ready to cook:

6 Remove the lamb from the marinade.

7 Thread the meat on to skewers, alternating with the onions.

8 Barbecue for 8-15 minutes, depending on how well done you like your lamb, turning often and basting with the left over marinade. Serve with Arabic bread and salad.

KOFTA KEBAB
Minced Meat on Skewers

*F*inely ground spiced minced meat is pressed on to long metal rods to be cooked over hot coals or in a tandoori oven. This is the Arabic equivalent to hamburgers. They may be found in street side stalls to be served with Arabic bread, some chopped lettuce and a rich strong sauce. They are ideal for barbecuing or grilling (broiling).

◄§ SERVES 4 §►

450 g / 1 lb / 1¼ cups minced (ground) lamb	5 ml / 1 tsp baharat (page 14)
2 onions, finely chopped	Pinch of cayenne pepper
30 ml / 2 tbsp parsley, chopped	Salt and pepper
30 ml / 2 tbsp chopped mint (or 15 ml / 1 tbsp dried)	Juice of 1 or 2 lemons

1 Combine the meat with all the other ingredients and mix to a smooth paste.

2 With oiled hands, press about 30 ml/2 tbsp of the lamb mixture tightly around one skewer, shaping into a sausage 12.5 cm/5 in long. Continue wrapping the remaining meat on to skewers.

3 Grill on a hot barbecue for 8-10 minutes, turning the skewers frequently. Serve with a sprinkling of lemon juice.

KIBDAH MESHWIA
Grilled Liver

L iver is another popular meat for the barbecue, and marinating it
for 30 minutes will help prevent it from drying out.

*A tomato or honey marinade is good (see page 105). In the
Levant a special dish called* kasbi meshwi bil tum *uses a
marinade of garlic paste, fresh chopped mint, olive oil, salt and
plenty of pepper.*

◆§ S E R V E S 4 – 6 §◆

450 g / 1 lb lambs' liver, cubed	Lemon slices
2 button (pearl) onions	Sprigs of fresh coriander (cilantro)
Arabic bread to serve	

1   Marinate the liver for 30 minutes if liked (see page 105).

2   Thread on to skewers alternating with the onions.

3   Grill (broil) over the barbecue for 4-5 minutes. This will cook the
liver, but leave the onions still a little crisp.

4   Garnish with lemon and coriander and serve with Arabic bread.

BATATES MASHWIYA FILFORN
Baked Potatoes

*B*aked potatoes to be eaten at a barbecue do seem to be a great favourite with so many nationalities that I decided to include them. Choose large, thick skinned potatoes that are free from 'eyes'.

Scrub well, prick the skin all over with a fork then sprinkle with salt and wrap in foil. They can then be put on the side of the barbecue at the start so that they heat up slowly and have time to cook right through. If you like a crisp skin remove the foil for the last 15 minutes, place over the hot charcoal turning once or twice.

AL KARKAND AL MASHWI
Roasted Corn on the Cob in Herb and Mustard Butter

*R*oasting the corn in the leaves ensures that all the flavours and juices are retained. Flavoured butters are a simple but effective way to add interest to plain food.

◄§ SERVES 8 §►

8 sweetcorn (corn) cobs	30 ml / 2 tbsp chopped shallots
HERB AND MUSTARD BUTTER	225 g / 8 oz / 1 cup butter
5 ml / 1 tsp French (Dijon) mustard	30 ml / 2 tbsp chopped (snipped) chives
10 ml / 2 tsp finely chopped parsley	10 ml / 2 tsp lemon juice

1 To make the butter, combine all the ingredients in a bowl and mix well. Cover and chill for 1-2 hours.

2 Just before you are ready to roast the corn, remove the outer leaves and all the silk, retaining two-thirds of the inner leaves. Liberally spread the herb butter over each cob, wrap them back in their leaves and then in the foil. Roast under a hot grill (broiler) or on glowing coals for about 10-15 minutes, turning frequently.

3 To serve, unwrap from the foil, remove the leaves, and serve with any remaining herb butter.

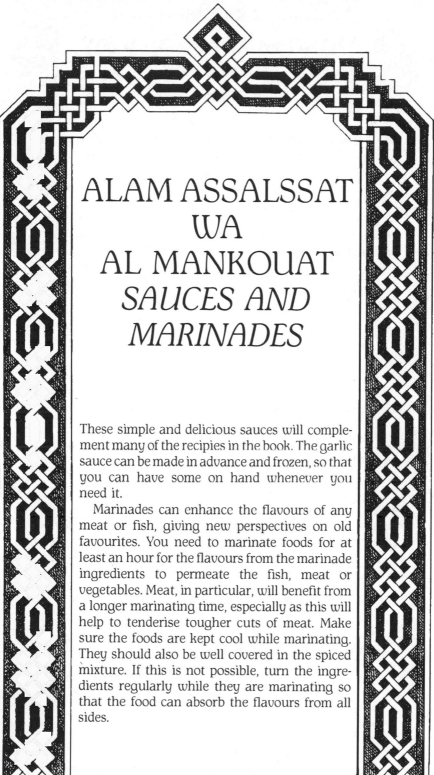

ALAM ASSALSSAT
WA
AL MANKOUAT
SAUCES AND
MARINADES

These simple and delicious sauces will comple-
ment many of the recipies in the book. The garlic
sauce can be made in advance and frozen, so that
you can have some on hand whenever you
need it.

Marinades can enhance the flavours of any
meat or fish, giving new perspectives on old
favourites. You need to marinate foods for at
least an hour for the flavours from the marinade
ingredients to permeate the fish, meat or
vegetables. Meat, in particular, will benefit from
a longer marinating time, especially as this will
help to tenderise tougher cuts of meat. Make
sure the foods are kept cool while marinating.
They should also be well covered in the spiced
mixture. If this is not possible, turn the ingredients regularly while they are marinating so
that the food can absorb the flavours from all
sides.

ATHOUM AL MOUKHALLAL
Garlic Sauce

*G*arlic must be one of the most important flavourings used in the whole of the Eastern world, and there are few savoury recipes where it is not present at some stage.

Raw garlic has a pungency that is removed by cooking or the addition of an egg yolk.

The sauce that follows is in two parts, and the first part may be used on its own. It may be made in large quantities, put into small pots and frozen. Wrap each frozen block in foil or cling film (plastic wrap), and store in a rigid container with a tight fitting lid. If the garlic is not very well wrapped the flavour will seep out into other foods.

With the addition of the egg yolk the garlic flavour becomes smoother and softer.

These quantities will be enough for many servings.

30–40 garlic cloves, crushed	Salt to taste
120 ml / 4 fl oz / ½ cup olive oil	1 egg yolk
90 ml / 6 tbsp lemon juice	120 ml / 4 fl oz / ½ cup olive oil

1 Put all the ingredients into a blender, adding a little water if necessary, and blend into a purée. If you do not have a blender reduce the garlic to a fine pulp using a garlic press or pestle and mortar. Add the oil and lemon juice slowly, beating well until all the ingredients are combined.

2 Beat the egg yolk with a whisk, then add the olive oil drop by drop until the mixture is thick. Add 5 ml/1 tsp of the garlic sauce and continue to whisk until well blended; a little water may be added to thin the sauce. Serve in small bowls.

ASSALSSA ALKHADRAE

Green Sauce for Prawns

*T*he colour of this sauce makes a lovely contrast to the pink of prawns (shrimp). It may also be served with any white fish. Serve chilled in a small bowl.

SERVES 6 - 8

75 g / 3 oz spinach leaves	600 ml / 1 pt / 2½ cups mayonnaise
50 g / 2 oz parsley	Pinch of cayenne pepper

1 Put the spinach leaves into boiling water for 4 minutes.

2 Strain and cool quickly by running under cold water. Pat dry with kitchen paper, although they do not have to be absolutely dry.

3 Pound the spinach and parsley into a pulp, or purée (blend) in a blender or food processor, then put through a sieve (strainer) to extract all the juices. Add the juice to the mayonnaise and add a pinch of cayenne pepper.

SALSSAT TARATOUR
Taratour Sauce with Pine Nuts

T his sauce is an ideal accompaniment to both seafood and vegetable dishes. It can also be used as a dip.

◆§ SERVES 4–6 §◆

25 g / 1 oz white bread with crusts removed	5 ml / 1 tsp salt
350 g / 12 oz pine nuts	250 ml / 8 fl oz / 1 cup lemon juice
2 garlic cloves, crushed	85 ml / 3 fl oz / 5½ tbsp water

1 Soak the bread then squeeze well.

2 Pound the pine nuts and the bread together to make a paste.

3 Add the garlic and salt and continue to pound the mixture, then add the lemon juice and water.

4 Strain if wished and place in a serving bowl. Chill well.

AL MANKOUAT
Marinades

*T*he purpose of a marinade is to tenderise and enhance the
flavour of meat or fish. If the meat is at all dry add a little oil
to the marinade.

Mankoue Al Hamed Bittawabil
Herb and Lemon

75 ml / 5 tbsp olive oil	Juice of 2 lemons
1 onion, sliced	1 carrot, sliced
1 celery stick (rib), chopped	1 sprig of parsley
1 bay leaf	15 ml / 1 tbsp each chopped thyme and parsley
6 peppercorns	

Mix all the ingredients together. Fish should be marinated for 20-30
minutes; chicken will need 1 hour or more.

Al Mankouat Al Jaffa
Dry Marinade

A dry marinade is made from crushed herbs and spices blended with salt
and garlic if liked, but do not use salt on uncooked beef as this causes
the juices to flow before the meat has been sealed by the heat.

Lahma Buharat
Marinade for Meat

1 onion, chopped	300 ml / ½ pt / 1¼ cups red wine vinegar
30 ml / 2 tbsp olive oil	1 carrot, chopped
8 juniper berries, crushed	4-6 peppercorns
Mixed herbs of your choice	

Mix all the ingredients together. For the mixed herbs a good choice
would be parsley, thyme and bay leaves, or use spicy aromatic salt (page 13).

Laban Buharat
Yoghurt-based Marinade

Excellent for a meat that might be a little tough. Crush a garlic clove and add to a large carton of natural (plain) yoghurt. Add 5 ml/1 tsp baharat (page 14), and the juice of half a lemon.

Or

Vary with different herbs and spices, such as coriander (cilantro), fennel, mint, saffron and baharat (page 14). Meat or poultry can be left in this overnight, fish is best left only a few hours. The marinade is used to baste the meat, fish or poultry while it is being cooked.

Chermoula Marinating Paste

Chermoula is a marinating paste originating from Morocco; it is used with fish and meat which will then be grilled (broiled).

1 onion	5 ml / 1 tsp pepper
2-4 garlic cloves	20 ml / 4 tsp paprika
2-4 red chillies)	5 ml / 1 tsp salt
30 ml / 2 tbsp chopped coriander (cilantro)	5 ml / 1 tsp saffron

Grind to a purée (paste) the onion, garlic, red chillies and the coriander. Add the remaining ingredients and mix well together. If necessary, a little oil may be added. To use, spread over the meat or fish and leave to marinate for at least 2 hours or overnight. Brush with a little oil then grill over charcoal, turning occasionally.

Dajaj Mankoue Fi Salssa Harra
Devilled Marinade for Chicken

120 ml / 4 fl oz / ½ cup light soy sauce	120 ml / 4 fl oz / ½ cup oil
3 spring onions (scallions), chopped	15 ml / 1 tbsp walnut oil
	30 ml / 2 tbsp clear honey
5 cm / 2 in piece of root ginger (gingerroot), grated	2 garlic cloves
	2.5 ml / ½ tsp allspice

Mix all the ingredients together then add the chicken, cover and keep overnight. When ready to cook remove from the marinade and dry well. Use the marinade to baste the chicken during cooking.

Attamatim Bi Mankoue
Honey Marinade for Meat

30 ml / 2 tbsp clear honey	Salt and pepper
1 large onion, grated	4 garlic cloves, crushed
5 ml / 1 tsp vinegar	5 ml / 1 tsp anchovies, finely chopped
5 ml / 1 tsp tamarind juice (page 13)	5 ml / 1 tsp lemon juice
Pinch of ground cloves	Pinch of cinnamon
30 ml / 2 tbsp oil	

Mix all the ingredients together and use as required. The anchovies and tamarind give this marinade a very strong flavour. If a milder flavour is preferred reduce the quantities or omit completely.

Assal Bi Mankoue
Tomato Marinade

A savoury and spicy tomato marinade suitable for meat, fish or chicken.

200 g / 7 oz / scant 2 cups tomato purée (paste)	2-3 garlic cloves, crushed
15 ml / 1 tbsp red wine vinegar or lemon juice	1 onion, finely chopped
	30 ml / 2 tbsp chopped parsley
2.5 ml / ½ tsp cinnamon	4 bay leaves
Salt and pepper	30 ml / 2 tbsp oil

Mix all the ingredients together, and use as required.

Buharat kabda
Marinade for Liver

15 ml / 1 tbsp chopped mint	1 garlic clove, crushed
15 ml / 1 tbsp grenadine syrup or pomegranate juice	5 ml / 1 tsp lemon juice
	Salt and pepper

Mix all the ingredients together and marinate the liver for 10-15 minutes The grenadine gives a very pleasant 'softness' to the flavour of the liver.

Samak Mubahar Belamoun Welashab
Herb and Lemon Marinade for Fish

75 ml / 5 tbsp olive oil	5 ml / 1 tsp salt
1 onion, grated	60 ml / 4 tbsp lemon juice
5 ml / 1 tsp chopped dill (dill weed) or fennel	5 ml / 1 tsp chopped parsley
	2.5 ml / ½ tsp dried thyme
6 peppercorns, crushed	1 bay leaf

Mix all the ingredients together and use as required.

Buharat Tabkah
Cooked Marinade

This is a sweet marinade using apricots as a base. It is particularly good with lamb, but it may also be used as a sauce to accompany other roast or grilled (broiled) meats.

3 onions, finely chopped	Salt and pepper
a little oil for frying	60 ml / 4 tbsp lemon or lime juice
2.5 ml / ½ tsp baharat (page 14)	1 garlic clove, crushed
2.5 ml / ½ tsp turmeric	2.5 ml / ½ tsp brown sugar
2.5 ml / ½ tsp ground coriander (cilantro)	15 ml / 1 tbsp apricot jam (conserve)

1 Fry (sauté) the onions in a little oil, add the baharat, turmeric, coriander, salt and pepper and fry for a further 2-3 minutes.

2 Add the lime or lemon juice with the garlic, brown sugar, apricot jam and 150 ml/¼ pt/⅔ cup water. Simmer for 15 minutes and leave to cool before using.

KHODAR
VEGETABLES

Buying vegetables in the open *souks* or market place is a delight to the eye and a pleasure not to be missed, though it is the men who do most of the shopping. The rows of stalls piled high with beautiful coloured fruit, vegetables and herbs are there to be chosen by the shopper and bargained for. The bargaining is done with enjoyment and humour. The vegetables or fruit are picked up one by one and examined and only the best are bought. The choice is extensive, including many that I have never come across before. The cucumbers are smaller than in the UK and the lime is in constant supply, but lemons may be used instead. Aubergines (eggplants) come in many sizes and colours, from the large deep purple and almost black to small thin pale mauve ones that are ideal for pickling. Parsley is of the continental flat leaf variety. Both the parsley and the coriander (cilantro) are in bunches that will weigh approximately 50-75 g/ 2-3 oz.

Vegetables form an important part of a meal for many of the Arabic peoples, whether in the form of a salad of tomatoes, cucumbers and onions or in the more elaborate casseroles.

Mishshi is the Arabic name for stuffed vegetables and is a great speciality of Middle Eastern cuisine. Many vegetables can be adapted this way and the stuffings can vary from meat and nuts to rice and other vegetables. They are all delicious and lovely to look at.

A word about aubergines (eggplants). I have come to the conclusion that the old wives' tale of cutting and salting aubergines to remove the bitter juices is very seldom necessary; having tested many varieties and sizes, I have found that in fact very few were bitter at all. I no longer do this prior to cooking them. However, I have included details of how to do this, should you prefer.

TABAK KHODAR AL ARMINIYA
Armenian Vegetable Casserole

This is an Armenian-style vegetable casserole using almost the same vegetables as the Moroccan Casserole on page 111, but its different method of cooking gives it a distinctly different flavour.

◄§ SERVES 4-6 §►

4 onions, quartered	60 ml / 4 tbsp chopped fresh mixed herbs
2 aubergines (eggplants), cubed	4 garlic cloves, chopped
4 carrots, cut into strips	Salt and pepper to taste
2 courgettes (zucchini), thickly sliced	30 ml / 2 tbsp oil
2 green (bell) peppers, diced	4 tomatoes, thickly sliced

1   Put all the prepared vegetables except the tomatoes into a large bowl with the mixed herbs, then add the garlic mashed with a little salt, pepper and oil.

2   Mix together well, then put into a casserole (Dutch oven), with a little stock or water, top with the tomatoes, cover and bake in the oven at 180°C/350°F/gas mark 4 for 40-50 minutes or until the vegetables are just tender.

TABAK AL MAGHRIBIYA
Moroccan-style Casserole

*T**he vegetables in this casserole are only a suggestion as the actual combination can be altered to suit the seasons. It would usually accompany a meat dish.*

❧ SERVES 4-6 ❧

900 ml / 1½ pt / 3¾ cups water or stock	1 aubergine (eggplant), cubed
Salt	3 courgettes (zucchini), cubed
3 carrots, sliced	45 ml / 3 tbsp oil
4-6 garlic cloves, sliced	1-2 chillies
3 onions, diced	5 ml / 1 tsp ground cumin
3 potatoes, cubed	30 ml / 2 tbsp chopped parsley
3 turnips, sliced	Salt and pepper to taste

1 Bring a large pan of salted water to the boil, add the carrots, garlic, 2 onions, potatoes, turnips and aubergines and bring back to the boil. Cover the pan and simmer for 15 minutes.

2 Add the courgettes and cook uncovered for 10 minutes more.

3 Meanwhile heat the oil and sauté the reserved onion, add the chillies, cumin and parsley and fry until the onions are soft.

4 Add the fried onion mixture to the vegetables and simmer for a further 5 minutes. Taste to adjust seasoning.

BADENJAN WYA CHOBAN
Aubergine Casserole

*T*his lovely dish from Syria has long been known as 'Shepherd's
Casserole'. It is an ideal meal for vegetarians and it is very
filling and nourishing. It is also very good eaten with roasted meats
or kebabs.

⋙ SERVES 4-6 ⋘

225 g / 8 oz firm white cheese
such as feta or haloumi,
grated or crumbled

2 eggs

15 ml / 1 tbsp milk

2.5 ml / ½ tsp salt

1.5 ml / ¼ tsp pepper

150 ml / ¼ pt / ⅔ cup oil

2 aubergines (eggplants), cut into
5 mm/¼ in slices

6 large tomatoes, sliced

60 ml / 4 tbsp chopped parsley

SAUCE

1 egg

5 ml / 1 tsp chopped (snipped)
chives

30 ml / 2 tbsp tomato purée (paste)

1 onion, chopped

2.5 ml / ½ tsp marjoram

Salt and pepper

1   Mix 30 ml/2 tbsp of the grated cheese with the eggs, milk, salt and
    pepper.

2   Heat the oil in a large frying pan (skillet).

3   Dip each of the aubergine slices into the egg and cheese mixture
    then fry (sauté) turning once until golden brown and soft. Remove
    and drain on kitchen paper.

4   Place half the aubergine slices on the base of a greased casserole
    (Dutch oven).

5   Cover with a layer of sliced tomatoes then sprinkle with half the
    remaining grated cheese and parsley. Repeat the layers.

6   Put the sauce ingredients into a bowl, blend well and pour evenly over the casserole. Bake in the oven at 180°C/350°F/gas mark 4 for about 45 minutes, or until the vegetables are cooked.

7   Remove from the oven and leave to cool for a few minutes before cutting into wedges.

FASOLYEH BI BANADOORA
Green Beans with Tomatoes

T his is a popular Middle Eastern vegetable dish and a great family favourite. It has one great advantage in that it is delicious whether it is served hot, warm or cold.

There are several varieties of green beans available, and all may be used in this recipe. As the cooking times will vary slightly, check them after 10 minutes.

SERVES 4 – 6

450 g / 1lb green beans	2.5 ml / ½ tsp allspice
120 ml / 4 fl oz / ½ cup oil	2 garlic cloves, crushed
1 large onion, chopped	2.5 ml / ½ tsp pepper
5 ml / 1 tsp salt	2 large tomatoes, coarsely chopped
30 ml / 2 tbsp lemon juice	

1   Wash the beans, and cut into 5 cm/2 in pieces.

2   Heat the oil in a large pan and fry (sauté) the onion until soft but not brown.

3   Add the beans, salt, allspice, garlic and pepper and stir fry for 5 minutes.

4   Add the tomatoes, the lemon juice and a little water, and cook covered for about 15 minutes, stirring occasionally, until the beans are tender and the liquid has thickened.

KHODARA MASH
Stuffed Vegetables

*T*o the Saudi Arabians and Gulf peoples, the Greeks and Turks, the North Africans, the Lebanese and all the other Middle Easterners, stuffed vegetables are party pieces and family favourites. Each country has developed its own speciality. The filling of vegetables was developed to titillate the palate and mystify the guests at court who tried to guess what these delightful stuffed vegetables contained. It might be a rich meat filling cooked in the best olive oil and tomato sauce or a blend of rice or burghul with nuts, fruit and other vegetables. Whatever their filling they were prepared by cooks who had great knowledge of food and a subtle way of combining flavours. The filled vegetables were first fried lightly in oil or butter before being stewed. But today with the trend for less rich and fattening foods the first frying may be omitted.

I have given the recipe for six fillings to fill about 1 kg/2 lb of vegetables; but it will, of course, depend on the size and the amount of pulp that is removed from each one. Each will serve abut six people.

General directions for stuffed vegetables

1 Prepare the stuffing of your choice (see below) as directed.

2 Remove the core of the vegetable to be stuffed with an apple corer or sharp knife. Leave a firm wall about 5 mm/¼ in thick, taking care not to pierce the skin. Rinse well. The removed flesh may be used as part of the filling or reserved for another recipe.

3 Carefully stuff the vegetables with the filling. If you have a filling of partly cooked rice do not pack it in tightly as the rice will expand.

4 Place the filled vegetables in a pan skin side down, add the liquid and simmer until cooked. They may also be cooked in a covered casserole (Dutch oven) in a moderate oven.

Fillings

Lahma wa Bouharat
Meat and Spice

15 ml / 1 tbsp oil or butter	1 garlic clove, crushed
1 onion, finely chopped	1.5 ml / ¼ tsp allspice
350 g / 12 oz lean beef or lamb, minced (ground) finely	Salt and pepper to taste
	50 g / 2 oz / ½ cup pine nuts

1 Heat the oil or butter in a pan and fry (sauté) the onion until soft and transparent.

2 Add the meat and garlic and fry until brown, add the seasonings and a little water or a mixture of tomato purée (paste) and water may be used. Continue to cook for a further 6–8 minutes.

3 Add the pine nuts. Leave the mixture to cool before using.

Lahma wa Rouz
Meat and Rice

Oil for frying	Salt and pepper
1 onion, chopped	100 g / 4 oz / ½ cup risotto rice, washed
225 g / 8 oz lamb or beef, minced (ground)	2-3 garlic cloves, crushed
30 ml / 2 tbsp chopped parsley	15 ml/ 1 tbsp lemon juice
2.5 ml / ½ tsp baharat (page 14)	30 ml/ 2 tbsp pine nuts

1 Fry (sauté) the onion in a little oil until just brown, add the meat and the rice and fry for 1-2 minutes.

2 Add the remaining ingredients with 120 ml/4 fl oz/½ cup of water and cook covered until the water has been absorbed.

3 As the rice will not be fully cooked, pack the filling in loosely.

Hamal wa Houmos
Lamb and Chick Peas

175 g / 6 oz lamb or beef, minced (ground)	100 g / 4 oz chick peas (garbanzos), cooked and roughly mashed
1 onion, finely chopped	1 garlic clove, crushed
15 ml / 1 tbsp parsley, chopped	

Cook the meat and onion as above, then add the chick peas and seasonings. Leave to cool before use.

Rouz Tomateur
Tomato Rice

1 large onion, chopped	2 large tomatoes, skinned and chopped
1 garlic clove, crushed	½ bunch of parsley, chopped
15 ml / 1 tbsp oil	2.5 ml / ½ tsp cinnamon
225 g / 8 oz / 1 cup risotto rice, washed	Salt and pepper
120 ml / 4 fl oz / 1 cup boiling water	

1 Fry (sauté) the onion and garlic in the oil until transparent.

2 Add the rice, tomatoes, parsley and cinnamon and fry for 1-2 minutes.

3 Add the boiling water, cover the pan and simmer gently until the liquid has been absorbed. Adjust the seasoning to taste. As the rice will be only half cooked, pack the filling loosely into the vegetables.

Hashwat Deek
Tomato and Burghul

50 g / 2 oz / ½ cup burghul	2-3 garlic cloves, chopped
3-4 onions, thinly sliced	5 large tomatoes, chopped
30 ml / 2 tbsp oil	45 ml / 3 tbsp chopped parsley
30 ml / 2 tbsp chopped mint	

1 Cover the burghul with boiling water and leave to stand for 15 minutes.

2 Fry (sauté) the onions in the oil until soft, add the garlic and tomatoes and cook for 1-2 minutes.

3 Add the remaining ingredients and the burghul. Mix well together. Leave to cool before use.

Moukh Hamal
Turkish Stuffing

175 g / 6 oz minced (ground) lamb	Salt and pepper
2 tomatoes, chopped	100 g / 4 oz / 1 cup Cheddar or Monteray Jack cheese, grated

1 Fry (sauté) the meat until browned then add the tomatoes, salt and pepper.

2 When the mixture is cool add the cheese and mix well together. This is particularly good for aubergines (eggplants) or courgettes (zucchini).

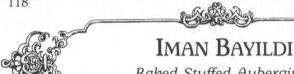

IMAN BAYILDI
Baked Stuffed Aubergines

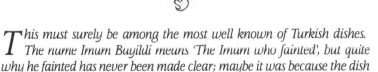

This must surely be among the most well known of Turkish dishes. The name Imam Bayildi means 'The Imam who fainted', but quite why he fainted has never been made clear; maybe it was because the dish his wife had just prepared was so good and yet so simple.

It can be served as a starter, in which case the aubergines are cut into small portions before serving, or served as a main course. Courgettes (zucchini) can replace the aubergines if you prefer.

◄§ SERVES 4–6 §►

2 aubergines (eggplants)	1 green (bell) pepper, finely chopped
Salt	2 tomatoes, peeled and chopped
120 ml / 4 fl oz / ½ cup olive oil	30 ml / 2 tbsp chopped parsley
2 onions, finely chopped	Juice of 1 lemon
2 garlic cloves, crushed	

1 Cut off the stems and wash the aubergines. Cut into half lengthways, then make a slit down the centre of each half, not right through to the skin. Salt each piece well and set aside for 30 minutes.

2 Rinse and drain and pat dry with kitchen paper.

3 Heat a little oil in a frying pan (skillet) then lightly brown the cut side of each half of the aubergines and set aside.

4 Add the remaining oil to the pan and fry (sauté) the onions, garlic and green pepper. Continue until the onions are soft then add the tomatoes and parsley and cook for 2-3 minutes. Season to taste.

5 Arrange the aubergine halves in a baking dish (pan) then put as much filling into each slit as possible.

6 Pour over the remaining oil, lemon juice and enough water to come half-way up the sides of the aubergines. Cover with foil or a lid and put into the top part of the oven at 190°C/375°F/gas mark 5 for about 1 hour; the aubergines should be soft and well cooked.

7 This dish is usually served cold.

BADHINJAN MAHSHI MA'LABAN
Stuffed Aubergines with Yoghurt

S mall aubergines are best for this recipe. If you use large ones, they will need a longer cooking time. Any cooking juices left at the end can be served as a separate accompaniment.

◆§ S E R V E S 6 §◆

12-14 small aubergines (eggplants)	1.5 ml / ¼ tsp cinnamon
Salt	2.5 ml / ½ tsp paprika
1 onion, chopped	Pepper
15 ml / 1 tbsp oil	30 ml / 2 tbsp tomato purée (paste)
1 kg / 2 lb lamb, minced (ground)	Knob of butter
30 ml / 2 tbsp finely chopped parsley	2 garlic cloves, crushed
30 ml / 2 tbsp pine nuts	Approximately 600 ml / 1 pt / 2½ cups natural (plain) yoghurt
1.5 ml / ¼ tsp chilli powder	

1   Wash and dry the aubergines, and cut off the stalks.

2   Scoop out the flesh, leaving a shell 5 mm/¼ in thick. Sprinkle with salt and leave to stand while making the filling.

3   Fry (sauté) the onions in the oil until brown, then add the meat. Continue to cook for another 5-10 minutes.

4   Add the parsley, pine nuts, spices and salt and pepper to taste, mix well together and remove from the heat.

5   Thoroughly rinse out the cored aubergines. Drain well and dry with kitchen paper. Fill with equal amounts of the meat mixture.

6   Place the aubergines in a pan, open end upwards.

7   Dilute the tomato purée in 450 ml/¾ pt/2 cups of water. Add a knob of butter and a pinch of salt and pepper, pour into the pan with the aubergines. See that the level of liquid reaches only about half way up the aubergines.

8 Bring quickly to the boil, cover and simmer for 40 minutes. Remove from the heat when cooked. This may also be cooked in the oven at 180°C/350°F/gas mark 4.

9 Add crushed garlic to the yoghurt with a little salt and serve separately.

Dukkous Al-tamat
Tomato Sauce

*T*he following sauce would add a richness if used for cooking the stuffed vegetables. It is especially good with aubergines (eggplants) and okra (ladies' fingers).

◄§ SERVES 4-6 §►

1 large onion, chopped	2 garlic cloves
15 ml / 1 tbsp olive oil	1.5 ml / ¼ tsp cinnamon
4 tomatoes, skinned and chopped	Salt and pepper
300 ml / ½ pt / 1¼ cups water	

1 Fry (sauté) the onion in olive oil until transparent.

2 Add the remaining ingredients and simmer for 15 minutes. The sauce may be puréed if liked.

BADHINJAN MASHI
Aubergines with Rice and Chick Peas

*T*he cooking time may vary depending on the type of rice and the size of the aubergines. Test them after about 45 minutes and continue cooking until they are tender.

◄§ SERVES 6 §►

6 aubergines (eggplants)	100 g / 4 oz / ½ cup risotto rice, washed and drained
Salt	
1 large onion, chopped	175 g / 6 oz / 1 cup chick peas (garbanzos), cooked and crushed
150 ml / ¼ pt / ⅔ cup oil	5 ml / 1 tsp cinnamon
225 g / 8 oz / 2 cups tomatoes, skinned and chopped	Pepper
	3 large tomatoes, sliced

1   Cut the stems from the aubergines and cut in half lengthways. Remove most of the flesh, but leave the shell about 5 mm/¼ in thick all round. Salt the inside and set aside while preparing the filling.

2   Fry (sauté) the onion in 15 ml/1 tbsp oil until soft but not brown. Put in a large bowl with the chopped tomatoes then add the rice, chick peas and cinnamon. Add salt and pepper and mix well together.

3   Rinse the aubergines and pat dry with kitchen paper then loosely pack with the rice mixture; remember that the rice will expand in the cooking.

4   Pour the remaining oil into a casserole (Dutch oven) then pack in the aubergines, cover with tomato slices and just enough water to come half way up the sides of the vegetables.

5   Cover the dish and cook in the oven at 180°C/350°F/gas mark 4 for 1 hour or until the aubergines and the rice are cooked through.

6   To serve as a main course keep hot and have a side salad and yoghurt to accompany it. Alternatively let it cool and serve as a side dish.

FILFIL AKHDAR MAHSHI
Green Peppers Stuffed with Spinach

*T*his colourful dish is a meal in itself. It is filling and nutritious,
ideal for a simple yet satisfying supper.

◆§ SERVES 4 §◆

4 green (bell) peppers	450 g / 1 lb / 8 cups spinach, washed and chopped
30 ml / 2 tbsp olive oil	1 cup cooked basmati rice (see page 133)
1 onion, diced	
2 garlic cloves, crushed	Salt and pepper

1   Cut the tops off the peppers and remove the seeds and pith. Heat the
    oil in a frying pan (skillet), add the peppers and lightly fry (sauté),
    turning them so that they are cooked all over. Remove from the pan
    and set aside.

2   Fry the onion and garlic until lightly browned.

3   Cook the spinach in a little salted water until soft. Drain and press
    out all the water.

4   Put the spinach into a large bowl, add the onions, garlic, rice and
    salt and pepper to taste, mix well together.

5   Spoon the mixture into the peppers, put on the tops and pack tightly
    into a baking dish (pan). Add a little water or stock to come a
    quarter of the way up the sides.

6   Cover and bake in the oven at 180°C/350°F/gas mark 4 for 30
    minutes.

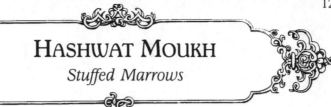

HASHWAT MOUKH
Stuffed Marrows

*T*he following filling is rich and spicy for a special occasion. Marrows are not frequently found in Middle Eastern markets but I thought as they are plentiful in Britain and the US in the summer months a recipe for them would not go amiss.

SERVES 4 – 6

1 large marrow (squash)	25 g / 1 oz / ¼ cup chopped almonds
15 ml / 1 tbsp oil	75 g / 3 oz / ½ cup chopped dried apricots soaked for 2 hours (or use ready-to-eat ones)
1 onion, chopped	
225 g / 8 oz lamb, finely minced (ground)	Salt and pepper
2.5 ml / ½ tsp baharat (page 14)	50 ml / 2 fl oz / 3½ tbsp water
50 g / 2 oz / ¼ cup risotto rice, washed and drained	

1 Wash the marrow and cut off the stalk, if any. Lay the marrow on its side and cut out a square piece in the centre and reserve. Scoop out all the seeds, leaving a wall of flesh.

2 Heat the oil and fry (sauté) the onion until lightly brown, add the meat and continue to fry until crumbly. Add the baharat, rice, almonds, the apricots and salt and pepper. Fry gently for 2 minutes then add the water.

3 Cook gently until all the liquid has been absorbed and the rice is half cooked. Cool slightly.

4 Fill the cavity of the marrow, replace the reserved section, like a lid, and place in a baking dish (pan).

5 Add enough water to come half way up the marrow and cook in the oven at 180°C/350°F/gas mark 4 for about 1 hour until cooked through. The time will depend on the size of the marrow.

BASAL BI SABANEGH
Onions and Spinach

*N*ever overcook spinach or it will go watery and lose its taste. This recipe gives its flavour a delicious lift. Serve it hot or cold with meat or poultry.

⋅§ SERVES 4 §⋅

450 g / 1 lb spinach	1 garlic clove, crushed
45 ml / 3 tbsp oil	2.5 ml / ½ tsp salt
2 onions, thinly sliced	1.5 ml / ¼ tsp pepper
Juice of 1 lemon	1.5 ml / ¼ tsp ground coriander (cilantro)

1   Wash the spinach very thoroughly, drain well and coarsely chop.

2   Cook the spinach in a little salted water for 5 minutes. Drain well and squeeze out excess moisture.

3   Heat the oil in a frying pan (skillet) and fry (sauté) the onions until they are soft and golden brown, remove half from the pan and set aside.

4   Add the lemon juice, garlic, salt, pepper and coriander to the onions in the pan, and mix together well.

5   Place the drained spinach on to a serving plate and spoon over the onion and garlic mixture.

6   Garnish with the remaining fried onions.

HIND BEH TAHINA
Swiss Chard Stems with Tahina

*T*he first time I was given this I did not recognise the vegetable
used. By the time I had finished enquiring there was total
confusion all round. I was finally shown a whole leaf and stalk, but
that did little to clear my confusion as I still did not recognise it at
all. On tasting the uncooked stalk the nearest equivalent flavour I
could think of was French sorrel. The Arabic name for the vegetable
was hind beh. I took the recipe home with me to experiment with
and decided that the larger stalks of spinach or the wider stalks of
Swiss chard gave a good substitute.

⋯§ SERVES 4 §⋯

450 g / 1 lb Swiss chard stems or spinach stems	50 ml / 2 fl oz / 3½ tbsp olive oil
1 large garlic clove	120 ml / 4 fl oz / ½ cup lemon juice
Salt to taste	25 g / 1 oz / ¼ cup chopped mint
225 g / 8 oz / 1 cup tahini	Paprika

1   Wash the stems well and cut into 2.5 cm/1 in lengths, and cook in
salted water until just tender. Drain well and pat dry.

2   Crush the garlic with the salt, add the tahini, then add the oil and
lemon juice a little at a time using a balloon whisk. If the mixture is
too thick add a little water, taste for seasoning.

3   Add the stems to the mixture and mix well. Put into a deep bowl
then sprinkle on the mint and a little paprika. Serve cold.

MIHSHI MALFUF
Stuffed Cabbage Leaves

*T*his dish needs careful preparation but it is worth the effort. You
could also cook the cabbage rolls in stock flavoured with
tomato purée (paste) and lemon juice.

•§ SERVES 4–6 §•

1 large cabbage	2.5 ml / ½ tsp allspice
30 ml / 2 tbsp oil	Salt and pepper
1 large onion, chopped	15 ml / 1 tbsp grenadine syrup
675 g / 1½ lb lamb, minced (ground)	50 ml / 2 fl oz / 3½ tbsp water
	2 garlic cloves, chopped
225 g / 8 oz / 1 cup risotto rice	5 ml / 1 tsp chopped mint

1   Remove the outer leaves of the cabbage carefully. The heart can be
used for a salad.

2   Boil the leaves a few at a time in salted water until just soft. Drain
and rinse in cold water.

3   If the leaves are very big they can be cut in half. If the stalks are
large, they can be either cut out or crushed with a rolling pin.

4   Heat the oil and gently fry (sauté) the onion and the meat, add the
rice, allspice and salt and pepper, and fry for 2 minutes.

5   Take 1 cabbage leaf and place upside down on a board, place 15 ml/
1 tbsp of filling on the bottom edge of the leaf and roll up, tucking
in the sides. Press with the hands to make a small, firm parcel.
Continue in this way until the filling is used up. Use any left over
leaves to line the base of a deep pan. Place the parcels on top of the
pieces of cabbage in the pan, packing them close together in layers.

6   Dilute the grenadine with the water and sprinkle the mixture
between each layer with half the chopped garlic and a little salt.

7   Crush the remaining garlic with the mint and sprinkle over the final
layer of cabbage rolls, then add just enough water to cover. Invert a
heavy plate on top of the rolls to keep them in place. Simmer on a
low heat for 1 hour. Serve with rice or potatoes.

TORSHI JAZAR BI SHUMMAR
Carrots with Fennel Seeds

*Y*ou can prepare the carrots how you prefer. The cooking time
will vary depending on size.

◄§ SERVES 4-6 §►

450 g / 1 lb carrots, peeled and sliced	30 ml / 2 tbsp oil
30 ml / 2 tbsp plain (all-purpose) flour	50 g / 2 oz / ¼ cup butter
Salt and pepper	250 ml / 8 fl oz / 1 cup natural (plain) yoghurt
	5 ml / 1 tsp fennel seeds

1   Boil the carrots in a little salted water until just cooked, drain and
leave to cool.

2   Put the flour, salt and pepper into a bag, add the carrots and toss to
coat.

3   Heat the oil and butter in a heavy pan and fry (sauté) the carrots on
both sides until lightly browned.

4   Meanwhile gently warm the yoghurt, transfer the carrots to a
serving dish and pour the yoghurt over them and sprinkle with the
fennel seeds.

LEFT
Turnips

*T*he Gulf Arabs consider that a turnip should be pink and
pickled, but in Tunisia they use young turnips sliced thinly,
soaked in olive oil, with the juice of a bitter orange or grapefruit
and a sprinkling of cayenne.

For those with rather a sweet tooth the following is very good.

SERVES 4-6

6 turnips, peeled and cubed	5-6 dates, stoned and mashed

Boil the turnips with the dates and a little water until soft. Drain well
and serve with a sprinkling of cinnamon.

KOUSSA MAHSHIYA
Stuffed Courgettes

*C*hoose courgettes (zucchini) that are even in size. Wash and cut
off the stem end and set aside. With the use of an apple corer
or a narrow sharp knife, scoop out the pulp, taking care not to cut
the skin. Choose a filling from pages 115-117 and fill the courgettes
with the stuffing. If a rice filling is used pack loosely. Lay the filled
courgettes in layers in a large pan and pour over the tomato sauce
(recipe on page 120) to just cover them. Simmer gently for 1 hour
or until the courgettes are soft and the filling cooked. A little
chopped mint may be added at the end of the cooking time.

The cores of the courgettes may be frozen for later use (or see
pages 129–130 for Courgette Rissoles or Fritters).

KOUSSA
Courgette Rissoles

*T*his was originally a Turkish recipe, and I have included it
   because it solves the problem of what to do with left over cores
from stuffed courgettes.

◄§ S E R V E S 4 §►

3 courgettes (zucchini)	15 ml / 1 tbsp chopped parsley
Salt and pepper	1 egg, lightly beaten
15 ml / 1 tbsp plain (all-purpose) flour	Breadcrumbs for coating
50 g / 2 oz / ¼ cup cottage cheese	Oil for deep frying

1   Thinly peel the courgettes, if liked, and grate them into a colander or
    sieve (strainer). Sprinkle with salt and leave to stand for 15-20
    minutes to drain.

2   Put the courgettes into a large bowl. Add the remaining ingredients
    except the breadcrumbs. Mix well.

3   Take walnut sized pieces of the mixture, roll them in breadcrumbs
    and deep-fry in the hot oil until crisp and golden. Drain on kitchen
    paper.

KOUSSA
Courgette Fritters

*T*his is an alternative to the previous recipe, using rather more eggs and a Cheddar or Monteray Jack cheese. They are fried flat like a pancake and are generally eaten as a snack or with the mezza.

❧ SERVES 6 ❧

450 g / 1 lb courgettes (zucchini)	60 ml / 4 tbsp cornflour (cornstarch)
3 eggs, beaten	100 g / 4 oz / 1 cup grated cheese
60 ml / 4 tbsp chopped mint	Salt and pepper

Oil for shallow frying

1   Grate the courgettes and put into a sieve (strainer) to drain.

2   Add the remaining ingredients and mix well.

3   Heat the oil and shallow fry (sauté) a spoonful at a time, pressing down to flatten. Brown on both sides and drain on kitchen paper.

HABOOB
GRAINS
AND PULSES

Due to the ease of storage, the seeds of certain plants, such as wheat, oats, rice, corn and rye have been for centuries a staple food in countries where drought is always possible. The Pharaohs in ancient times had small vessels of grain buried with them in their tombs.

Pulses are also a valuable addition to any diet. There are many varities of beans and they are all extremely valuable nutritionally. They are high in fibre, proteins and minerals and low in fats, and do not contain any cholesterol.

Beans need to be thoroughly cooked to break down the starch and thus aid digestion. If eating beans causes a problem with wind, soaking the beans in plenty of water prior to cooking will help. Change the water frequently and do not use the soaking water to cook the beans. The addition of a pinch of asafetida will also help. In India it is valued for its truffle-like flavour and a pinch or two is always added to a pot of beans or lentils.

There are many types of rice available on the market, the best of which is probably Basmati which is grown in India and Pakistan. This is a thin, long grain with the most superb flavour and does not take long to cook. The other long grain variety is Patna from India. There are also the quick cooking varieties, but they do not have the flavour of Basmati.

Rice has been measured by volume here, as I think this is the easiest method. There are two basic methods of cooking, and both are given here.

ATTARIKA AL ADIYA LITAHYI AL ORZ
Plain Rice by Absorption

*T*his method of cooking will produce rice with the greatest
flavour. Choose a pan with a well-fitting lid, and if it will go
into the oven so much the better. Keep an eye on the timing
because rice is not a food that you can put on and leave. It is better
to use too little water than too much. If using basmati rice, reduce
the amount of water slightly. Always wash the rice first to remove
excess starch.

◄§ S E R V E S 4 §►

....
2 cups rice, washed thoroughly   4 cups water
....

1   Wash the rice and soak for 15–20 minutes. This will reduce the
    cooking time slightly.

2   Bring the water to the boil in a heavy pan. Drain the rice, add to the
    water, stirring once, and put on the lid. As soon as the water comes
    back to the boil lower the heat.

3   Leave for 8 minutes before testing. If the water has been absorbed
    and the grains are not brittle in the centre, turn off the heat and
    leave to stand with the lid on, or put the pan into a warm oven on
    the lowest setting. If the grains are still brittle add a little more
    boiling water and cook for a further 3 minutes before testing again.

4   Once cooked, leave to stand for 10 minutes so that the grains will
    fluff out and separate.

•   275 g/10 oz is equivalent to 2 teacups of dry rice, enough for about 4
    servings. If using American cups 1 cup holds about 8 oz dry rice. Use
    twice the volume of water to rice whatever cup size you use.

AL ORZ
Plain Boiled Rice

*T*he cooking of rice varies from person to person. This is a
straightforward method that does not impart all the flavour of
the absorption method but nevertheless makes a suitable
accompaniment to any meal.

◄§ S E R V E S 4 §►

. . . .
2 cups Basmati or long grain rice
. . . .

1   Wash the rice well, with the final rinse being of hot water. Drain
well.

2   Put plenty of water and a pinch of salt into a large pan and bring to
the boil. Add the rice, stirring now and again, then bring back to the
boil. Lower the heat slightly and boil gently for 10-15 minutes. Test a
grain or two; if the centre is no longer brittle put the rice into a
strainer to remove as much water as possible. Put the strainer on to
a dry tea towel (dish cloth) to remove the last traces of moisture. It
may be served now or it can stand in a warm place to dry out and
expand.

ORZ BI ASSIR ARROMAN
Rice and Grenadine

*T*he authentic version of this recipe uses pomegranate juice but
as this might be hard to buy, grenadine syrup can be used
instead. It is a slightly sweet dish with an interesting flavour and is
delicious served with chicken or a vegetable dish. Roasted chicken
legs are sometimes served with it.

◆§ SERVES 4 §◆

6 onions, chopped	2 cups risotto rice
45 ml / 3 tbsp oil	75 g / 3 oz / ¾ cup chopped walnuts
1 l / 1¾ pts / 4¼ cups water	
120 ml / 4 fl oz / ½ cup grenadine syrup	Salt and pepper

1   Fry (sauté) the onions in the oil until transparent. Add the water and
the grenadine syrup and bring slowly to the boil.

2   Add the rice and walnuts. Cook until the water has evaporated, fluff
up with a fork and season to taste.

3   Put the lid back on the saucepan and heat over a low flame for 10
minutes. A delicious crust will form on the bottom.

ORZ BILLAWNI
Coloured Rice

*C*oloured rice not only adds greatly to the visual pleasure of food, it also enhances the flavour of the rice.

Orz Billawni Al Akhdar Walahmar
Green rice
Add fresh chopped herbs such as parsley, fresh coriander (cilantro), chives or, most popular in the Arab world, mint to the rice when it has finished cooking and fluff up with a fork.

Orz Billawni Al Akhdar Walahmar
Red rice
Add tomato purée (paste) to the cooking water or a few chopped tomatoes may be added at the end.

Orz Billawni Al Assfar
Yellow rice
The saffron imparts a most lovely fragrance and flavour to the rice. Turmeric may be used instead in small quantities. To give a patchwork effect saffron can be added to the rice in small pockets, left for a few minutes then gently fluffed up. To colour evenly, add a few grains of saffron or turmeric to the water at the start of cooking.

Rouz Bassal
Onion rice
Mounds of onion rice are a popular accompaniment to many dishes. Chopped onions fried (sautéed) in butter are added to the rice while it is cooking. Two or three more onions are then sliced and fried until crisp and golden, then sprinkled on to the cooked rice.

Rouz Fawakeh wa Bouzoorat
Rice with fruit and nuts
For over 5,000 years Arabs have sun-dried fruit, mainly dates as these grow freely in the oases, but also figs, raisins and many other fruits. Apricots are also popular. These must have come from China with the caravans on their long treks through the deserts.

Chop the fruit to be used into small pieces and roughly chop the nuts. Add to the rice and cook by absorption. A little more water may be necessary. Good combinations would be apricots and almonds, dates with cinnamon and a little baharat (page 14) to add spice, walnuts and raisins, or pomegranate seeds on their own.

HARISS
Wheat Dish

W heat, thought to have first been cultivated in the regions of the Nile, is the basis of this wholesome dish. Hariss means 'well cooked', an excellent description as the wheat is usually puréed. Occasionally it is added to a little minced lamb or chicken. This is the Arabic form of porridge, popular with children with a little honey poured over it. There is another version where the wheat is cooked in a lamb stock, with a little cinnamon added.

SERVES 4–6

350 g / 12 oz / 3 cups whole wheat grains	5 ml / 1 tsp cinnamon
7.5 ml / 1½ tsp salt	30 g / 1 oz / 2 tbsp butter
	Melted butter to serve

1   Soak the grain overnight in water, rinse and drain.

2   Boil the wheat in salted water to cover for about 3-4 hours or until soft. Remove any scum as it rises.

3   Add the cinnamon and seasoning to taste and blend to a purée.

4   Serve with a spoonful of melted butter.

BURGHUL
Cracked Wheat

*W*hole wheat grains are boiled, dried and finally roughly ground to form burghul. It is sold in three grades of fine, medium and coarse. It is a prominent food throughout the Middle East and forms the basis of tabouleh, *and many of the* kibbeh *recipes. Burghul may replace rice in many of the recipes. To cook, always use an equal quantity of grain to water so a cup measure is best. Any cup will do, but use the same one for the grain and water.*

◄§ SERVES 4–6 §►

225 g / 8 oz / 2 cups coarse burghul wheat	5 ml / 1 tsp salt
450 ml / ¾ pt / 2 cups water or stock	Melted butter to serve

1 Bring the stock or water to the boil, and add the salt and burghul.

2 Cover the pan with a lid and simmer gently for 10-15 minutes or until tender. The liquid should all have been absorbed.

3 Pour a little melted butter over the grains and leave to stand for 5-10 minutes.

Variation
• 45 ml/3 tbsp fried pine nuts or slivered almonds or raisins may be added at the end of the cooking time.

Couscous
Couscous

*D*urum or hard wheat is the basis for making couscous. It is spread out into even sized grains which are covered in flour then steamed and dried. It is in this form that it can be bought in the shops as semolina (cream of wheat). It will need a further steaming over a stew of meat or chicken to impart some flavour into the grains.

This is a speciality of Morocco and other North African countries. It is eaten in a savoury or a sweet form. A couscousier is a special steamer for cooking the couscous, but an ordinary sieve (strainer) that will fit closely over a deep pan will do. The strainer should not touch the stock below as the grain should be steamed.

1   Spread out the required amount of couscous on to a large tray and sprinkle with a little water and salt. Fork through or use your fingers to loosen the grains.

2   Using a large deep pan, put in the meat or vegetables and the stock. Bring to the boil and simmer until nearly cooked.

3   If you do not have a couscousier use a sieve that will fit over the pan, lined with muslin if the holes are large. Put in a small amount of couscous and the snugly fitting lid to ensure that no steam escapes. When the steam is flowing add the remaining couscous and the lid. Fork through occasionally to ensure that the grains do not stick together.

4   Arrange the couscous on a large plate and make a hole in the centre. Spoon in the meat and vegetables. Serve the sauce separately.

MASRUA SALATAT FASOULIA
Egyptian Bean Salad

*T*his is generally known as an Egyptian bean salad as it is made
with the brown beans that are so popular in Egypt. This dish is
similar to the ful medames recipe, but the cooking time is
considerably less and a lot simpler, though it is just as delicious.
Substitute other dried beans if you prefer. As this recipe improves
with keeping, cook the day before it is required.

◄§ SERVES 6 §►

450 g / 1 lb / 2⅔ cups Egyptian
brown beans, soaked overnight
and drained

15 ml / 1 tbsp parsley, chopped

60 ml / 4 tbsp olive oil

Salt and pepper

2 garlic cloves, crushed

Juice of 1 lemon

1   Cover the beans in cold water, bring slowly to the boil, boil rapidly
for 10 minutes then simmer for about 1½ hours or until tender.
Allow them to cool, then drain.

2   Mix the remaining ingredients together and pour over the beans.
Toss gently and check the seasoning, adding more olive oil and
lemon juice if necessary.

TABAQ FASOULI ARABI
Arabian Bean Pot

*T*he beans in this recipe can be the dried lima, chick peas
*(garbanzos) or any beans of your choice. The rather sour
variety of cooking apples are best as their flavour contrasts so well
with the apricots. This is a delicious and nutritious dish.*

◄§ S E R V E S 6 – 8 §►

450 g / 1 lb dried beans, soaked overnight	2.5 ml / ½ tsp turmeric
30 g / 1 oz / 2 tbsp oil or butter	300 ml / ½ pt / 1¼ cups natural (plain) yoghurt
2 onions, sliced	50 g / 2 oz / ⅓ cup chopped dried apricots (soaked for 2 hours or use the ready-to-eat variety)
2 cooking (tart) apples, cored and sliced	
5 ml / 1 tsp cinnamon	

1   Drain and rinse the beans; put into a heavy pan, cover with water
and bring slowly to the boil. Boil rapidly for 10 minutes, then
simmer for 1½ hours or until the beans are tender.

2   Heat the oil in a large, heavy frying pan (skillet) and fry (sauté) the
onions until golden. Add the apples and spices and continue to cook,
stirring gently, until the apple is half cooked.

3   Add the beans with about 250 ml/8 fl oz/1 cup of the liquid and
continue to cook until the apple is soft.

4   Beat the yoghurt until creamy then add the chopped apricots. The
beans may be served warm with the yoghurt sauce.

HOMMOS HAR
Spiced Chick Peas

*Y*ou can speed up this recipe by using drained canned chick
peas. The dish can be eaten hot or cold.

◄§ SERVES 4-6 §►

225 g / 8 oz / 1⅓ cups chick peas (garbanzos), soaked overnight	1 red or green (bell) pepper, finely chopped
30 ml / 2 tbsp oil	15 ml / 1 tbsp tomato purée (paste)
2 onions, finely chopped	300 ml / ½ pt / 1¼ cups stock from cooking the beans
5 ml / 1 tsp ground coriander (cilantro)	30 ml / 2 tbsp lemon juice
5 ml / 1 tsp grated root ginger (gingerroot)	15 ml / 1 tbsp chopped coriander (cilantro)
5 ml / 1 tsp ground cumin	Salt and pepper

1   Put the chick peas into a large saucepan and cover with cold water,
     bring to the boil and boil rapidly for 10 minutes, removing the scum
     when necessary. Lower the heat and simmer until the beans are
     cooked. When tender drain off the cooking liquid, but reserve
     300 ml/½ pt/1¼ cups.

2   Meanwhile heat the oil in a large pan and gently fry (sauté) the
     onions with the spices for 5-7 minutes, add the diced peppers and the
     cooked chick peas.

3   Dissolve the tomato purée in 150 ml/¼ pt/½ cup of the bean water
     and add to the beans, stir frequently and cook gently with the lid on
     for 10 minutes.

4   Add the lemon juice, the chopped coriander and adjust the
     seasoning. The remaining sauce should be thick and form a coating
     for the chick peas.

FASOULIA
White Haricot Bean Stew

I have also cooked this recipe with chick peas and have found *them an excellent alternative to haricot beans. It can be eaten hot or cold.*

⋖§ S E R V E S 4 – 6 §⋗

225 g / 8 oz / 1⅓ cup haricot (navy) beans, soaked overnight	5 ml / 1 tsp dried oregano
1 small clove of garlic	30 ml / 2 tbsp tomato purée (paste)
120 ml / 4 fl oz / ½ cup olive oil	Salt and pepper
1 bay leaf	Juice of 1 lemon
	½ small onion, diced

1 Put the beans into a large, heavy pot, add the garlic, peeled and well crushed, the oil, bay leaf and oregano and stir fry gently for 15 minutes.

2 Remove from the heat and carefully pour in enough boiling water to just cover the beans. Stir in the tomato purée. Bring to the boil, reduce the heat and simmer covered on a very low heat for 2-3 hours. When the beans are tender add salt and pepper, sprinkle on the lemon juice and serve garnished with the raw onion.

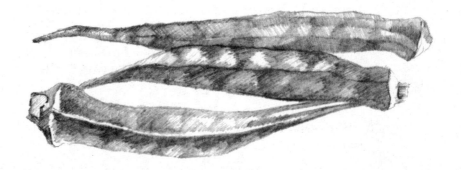

TORSHI
PICKLES

In certain parts of the Arabic world such as the Arabian Gulf, there used to be long periods when it was impossible to grow fresh fruit and vegetables. People would live on a diet consisting mainly of meat and dates, rice when it could be bought from a passing caravan and milk from their camels and goats. So to give variety to an otherwise limited diet, they pickled fruit and vegetables when they were abundant. An Arabic kitchen could be a colourful place with a large array of stacked pickle jars. Almost any fruit or vegetable was pickled either raw or cooked, depending on the type.

When choosing your vegetables or fruit, buy fresh and unblemished. Some will need cutting and blanching.

The brine used may vary in the proportions of salt to water and water to vinegar. It really depends on the length of time they are to be kept. For brine it is recommended that you use 30-40 ml/2-3 tbsp salt to each 600 ml/1 pint/2½ cups water and for vinegar pickling 600 ml/1 pint/2½ cups vinegar to the same amount of water. Too little salt in the brine or vinegar in the solution will not prevent micro-organisms from forming and too much will spoil the flavour.

One of the most popular varieties is turnips that have been pickled with slices of beetroot, and have therefore turned a delicate shade of pink. There are also the rich and succulent aubergines (eggplants), pickled cloves of garlic, orange and lemon peel, limes, apricots and mangos.

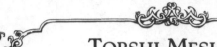

TORSHI MESHAKEL
Mixed Pickles

*T*hese and the following pickles are generally not over-spiced. If you like your pickles hotter, you can add a chilli or two to any of them. Serve them in small bowls to accompany any meat or fish dishes.

◄§ MAKES 1 kg / 2 lb §►

4 cucumbers	PICKLING BRINE
2 carrots	600 ml / 1 pt / 2½ cups white vinegar
1 cauliflower	
1 green (bell) pepper	600 ml / 1 pt / 2½ cups cold water
4 turnips	30 ml / 2 tbsp salt
15 green beans	10 ml / 2 tsp sugar
3 garlic cloves	
1 chilli	
1 sprig dill (dill weed)	

1 Prepare the vegetables by washing and cutting into lengths or, in the case of cauliflower, into small florets. Dry on kitchen paper then pack into sterilised jars.

2 Bring the pickling brine to the boil and cook on a high heat for 2 minutes, leave to cool.

3 Pour the brine over the packed vegetables until the jars are full. Shake gently to remove all the bubbles. Seal.

4 Store in a cool, dark place. If settling has occurred after 2 days, add more brine.

5 Leave to pickle for 2 weeks before eating.

TORSHI BEDENJAN
Aubergine Pickle

*T*hese are delicious but very rich, so I would cut one aubergine into slices and serve it in a small bowl. If you cannot buy very small aubergines, increase the quantity of filling for each one and increase the initial cooking time by 5-8 minutes. If you are short of olive oil, use half olive oil and half sunflower oil.

8-10 very small aubergines (eggplants)	30 ml / 2 tbsp finely chopped parsley
3-4 chillies	8 garlic cloves
1 large handful of walnuts, coarsely chopped	10 ml / 2 tsp salt
	Olive oil

1 Wash the aubergines and trim off the stalks. Make a lengthwise slit down each aubergine to form a small pocket.

2 Boil the aubergines in lightly salted water for 3 minutes, remove them and drain well.

3 Place the aubergines in a colander or sieve (strainer) and cover with a plate. Leave them overnight to drain the juices.

4 To make the stuffing, finely chop the chillies and mix together with the walnuts, parsley, crushed garlic and salt. Stuff this mixture into the slit in each aubergine. For a milder flavour remove the seeds from the chillies.

5 Pack the stuffed aubergines into a sterilised wide pickling jar; completely fill the jar with olive oil and cover with an airtight lid.

6 Leave to stand at room temperature for at least two weeks.

TORSHI FILFIL
Pickled Chillies

*P*ickled chillies are full of flavour and easy to prepare. They are particularly good with fish dishes.

450 g / 1 lb small green and red chillies	10 ml / 2 tsp sugar
600 ml / 1 pt / 2½ cups white vinegar	2.5 ml / ½ tsp salt

1   Wash and dry the chillies and pack into sterilised jars.

2   Mix the remaining ingredients and bring to the boil. Cook on a high heat for 2 minutes, then leave to cool. Fill the jars with the liquid then shake gently to remove air bubbles. Seal.

3   Store in a cool, dark place. After 3-4 days add more vinegar solution if necessary. Leave for 2 weeks. The vinegar will have absorbed the flavour from the chillies so when serving add a little of the liquid with the chillies.

TORSHI LEFT
Pickled Turnips

*T*his pickle is pleasing to the eye as well as to the palate, as the beetroot turns the turnips pink. Serve to accompany meat or fish dishes.

1 kg / 2 lb white turnips	1.2 l / 2 pts / 5 cups water
1 raw beetroot, peeled and sliced	600 ml / 1 pt / 2½ cups white vinegar
3 garlic cloves	30 ml / 2 tbsp salt

1 Peel and wash the turnips, cut them into quarters and pack into sterilised jars, adding pieces of beetroot between the layers of turnips. Add the garlic.

2 Bring the water and vinegar to the boil, add the salt and boil for 5 minutes. When cool fill sterilised jars, shake gently to remove air bubbles and seal.

3 Store the jars in a cool, dark place. The pickles will be ready in 2 weeks.

ACHAR BANADURA
Pickled Tomatoes

S erve to accompany meat or fish dishes. Make sure you use firm fruit or the results will be disappointing.

1 kg / 2 lb small, firm tomatoes	10 ml / 2 tsp ground coriander (cilantro)
30 ml / 2 tbsp salt	6 garlic cloves
15 ml / 1 tbsp pepper	900 ml / 1½ pt / 3¾ cups white vinegar
15 ml / 1 tbsp paprika	

1 Wash the tomatoes and dry. At the top of each tomato make a cross with a sharp pointed knife and fill with salt. Place them upside down on a plate for 2 hours to drain.

2 Mix the pepper, paprika and coriander and put into each tomato. Pack them into wide sterilised jars, alternating with layers of garlic.

3 Cover the tomatoes with vinegar. Shake gently to remove air bubbles. Seal. Leave for 1 week in a cool, dark place before using.

MUROBA LEMON WA PORTUCAL
Lemon or Orange Peel Preserve

These preserves do not usually accompany food. They are passed round as a sweetmeat, often to the ladies as they are drinking their coffee.

6 oranges or lemons	2 cardamoms, cracked
30 ml / 2 tbsp lemon juice	300 ml / ½ pt / 1¼ cups water
675 g / 1½ lbs / 3 cups sugar	30-45 ml / 2-3 tbsp rose water

1 Remove the rind from the oranges and lemons in strips and scrape off any of the white pith. The flesh may be used for a fruit salad.

2 Soak the rind in cold water for 12 hours.

3 Simmer the rind in some fresh water for 30 minutes, adding more water as necessary. Drain.

4 Mix the lemon juice, sugar and cardamoms with the measured amount of water and bring to the boil. Add the rind and simmer for 30 minutes. Leave to cool, then add the rose water.

5 Fill the jars with the rind and the cooking liquid. Seal. Leave to stand for 2 weeks in a cool, dark place.

ATHOUM AL HAR
Pickled Garlic

Soak whole or lightly crushed, peeled garlic cloves in vinegar for a week to serve with a meat dish or add to cooked dishes requiring a strong garlic flavour.

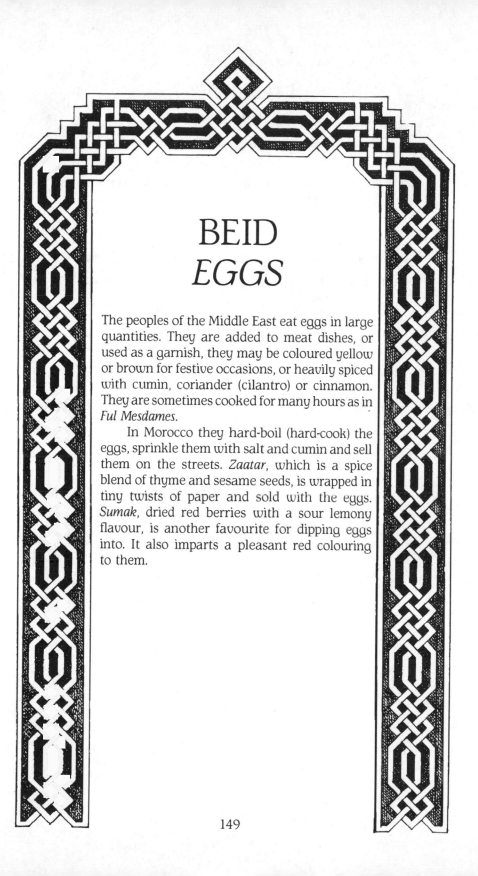

BEID
EGGS

The peoples of the Middle East eat eggs in large quantities. They are added to meat dishes, or used as a garnish, they may be coloured yellow or brown for festive occasions, or heavily spiced with cumin, coriander (cilantro) or cinnamon. They are sometimes cooked for many hours as in *Ful Mesdames.*

In Morocco they hard-boil (hard-cook) the eggs, sprinkle them with salt and cumin and sell them on the streets. *Zaatar*, which is a spice blend of thyme and sesame seeds, is wrapped in tiny twists of paper and sold with the eggs. *Sumak*, dried red berries with a sour lemony flavour, is another favourite for dipping eggs into. It also imparts a pleasant red colouring to them.

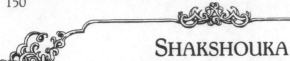

SHAKSHOUKA
Eggs with Tomatoes

With crisp French bread and a salad, this would make an appetising lunch.

≈§ SERVES 4 §≈

1 onion, sliced	4 small tomatoes, sliced
½ green (bell) pepper, diced	4 eggs, beaten
30 g / 1 oz / 2 tbsp oil or butter	Salt and pepper
Chopped parsley	

1 Fry (sauté) the onions and peppers in the oil or butter then add the tomatoes and simmer until the onions are soft.

2 Scramble the eggs, adding salt and pepper to taste.

3 Add the scrambled eggs to the tomato mixture and stir gently to combine the ingredients.

4 Serve with the parsley sprinkled on the eggs.

BEID BI LABAN
Poached Eggs in Yoghurt

This egg dish is rather strange to many Western tastes. Don't be afraid to try it though because it is surprisingly good served as a light meal or supper dish.

≈§ SERVES 4 §≈

4 eggs	30 g / 1 oz / 2 tbsp butter
450 ml / ¾ pt / 2 cups natural (plain) yoghurt	5 ml / 1 tsp paprika
2 garlic cloves, crushed	Salt and pepper

1 Poach the eggs in an egg poacher or a pan of simmering water with a little lemon juice added until the whites are set but the yolks still soft.

2 Beat the yoghurt and garlic together then divide into four individual bowls. Melt the butter and add the paprika, stir well.

3 Slip a hot poached egg into each bowl of yoghurt, pour over some of the butter and paprika, add salt and pepper to taste.

4 Serve immediately.

BID MAA ASSABANIGH

Eggs with Spinach

S erve this with crusty bread for a light lunch. Be careful not to overcook the spinach or the finished dish will be watery.

⋖§ SERVES 4 §⋗

50 g / 2 oz / ¼ cup butter	4 eggs
1 onion, finely sliced	Salt and pepper
450 g / 1 lb spinach, washed and chopped	

1 Melt the butter in a heavy baking dish (pan) and fry (sauté) the onions until soft.

2 Add the spinach and cook over a low heat until wilted and soft.

3 Spread the spinach evenly over the base of the dish, then carefully break the four eggs on to the spinach, spacing them evenly.

4 Put on a lid and cook gently until the eggs are set. Season well and serve at once.

BEID MUTAJJAN
Fried Hard-boiled Eggs

E gyptian street vendors are well known for selling hard-boiled (hard-cooked) eggs with a surprise parcel of spices rolled up in twists of newspaper. The tiny parcel is opened to reveal a thyme and sesame seed blend called zaatar, *or* duka, *which is a mixture of ground hazelnuts or peanuts, or the more simple and usual cumin and salt.*

A recipe from medieval times records a variety of spices used to coat fried hard-boiled eggs.

◄§ S E R V E S 4 §►

4 hard-boiled (hard-cooked) eggs	10 ml / 2 tsp ground cumin
30 ml / 2 tbsp oil	5 ml / 1 tsp ground coriander (cilantro)
10 ml / 2 tsp cinnamon	Salt and pepper
2.5 ml / ½ tsp turmeric	

1 Shell the eggs and prick small holes in the whites. This will prevent the eggs from splitting and enhance the flavours.

2 Lightly fry (sauté) the whole eggs in the oil until they are just coloured. Drain.

3 Combine the spices and roll each egg into the mixture.

4 Serve for breakfast or as a garnish.

Variation
• Instead of the spices used in the above recipe, the egg can be fried with crushed garlic then sprinkled with lemon juice and chopped mint.

BEID MASHI
Stuffed Eggs

*T*hese eggs could form part of the Mezza or be added to a salad.
The method is quite fiddly but well worth the effort as the
finished dish is delicious.

◄§ SERVES 4 §►

4 hard-boiled (hard-cooked) eggs, shelled and cut in half	45 ml / 3 tbsp olive oil
15 ml / 1 tbsp parsley, finely chopped	2.5 ml / ½ tsp cinnamon
1 onion, finely chopped	Salt and pepper
	Lettuce leaves
	Pinch of paprika

1 Cut the eggs in half carefully. Remove the yolks and put into a bowl, mash with a fork then mix in the parsley and onion. Add the olive oil a drop at a time.

2 Add the cinnamon and salt and pepper and mix well together.

3 Take a spoonful of the mixture to fill one half of an egg white. Continue in this way until all the mixture is used up and the egg whites are filled.

4 Arrange the eggs on a bed of lettuce leaves and sprinkle with paprika.

5 If liked, serve with a dressing or a yoghurt sauce.

EJJAH
Omelettes

*A*rabic omelettes are a far cry from the light, fluffy affairs of the French ones. The proportion of filling to egg is quite the reverse. They are rather like a Spanish omelette in so far as the finished product may be eaten hot or cold and served cut into wedges similar to a cake. The eggs hold the ingredients together.

The ejjah should be cooked slowly and evenly either on top of the stove or in an oven, both methods needing well fitting lids. The utensil used should not be too large as the finished ejjah should be 3-5 cm/1½-2 in thick.

EJJAH BILJOZ
Walnut Omelette

*T*his snack is a tasty combination of sweet and savoury ingredients and provides an interesting texture too. Serve hot as a snack.

SERVES 4

6 eggs, beaten	100 g / 4 oz / 1 cup chopped walnuts
50 g / 2 oz / ⅓ cup washed currants	15 ml / 1 tbsp chopped (snipped) chives
2.5 ml / ½ tsp turmeric	60 ml / 4 tbsp breadcrumbs
Salt and pepper	Oil for frying

1 Combine all the ingredients except the oil, and mix them together well.

2 Heat the oil in a heavy frying pan (skillet) and pour in the egg mixture. Cook over a low heat, turn and brown on the other side. Serve immediately.

EJJAH KHODAR
Vegetable Omelette

*T*hese quantities will serve 2 people as a supper dish. The
ingredients may easily be doubled for either a main course or
for more people.

◄§ S E R V E S 2 §►

1 onion, roughly chopped	1 tomato, chopped
30 ml / 2 tbsp oil	1 potato, cooked and diced
1 garlic clove, crushed	2 sprigs of parsley, chopped
2 courgettes (zucchini), cut into small cubes	15 ml / 1 tbsp mint, chopped
1 green (bell) pepper, diced	Salt and pepper
	4 eggs

1 Fry the onion in the oil until lightly coloured, add the garlic,
   courgettes, pepper and tomato. Cook these gently with the lid on the
   pan until nearly soft. Add a little water if necessary.

2 Remove from the heat and add the potato, herbs and salt and pepper
   to taste.

3 Beat the eggs lightly in a large bowl, then add the vegetables,
   stirring them to combine well with the eggs.

4 Pour the mixture into a hot oiled heavy frying pan (skillet), cover
   with a lid or plate and cook slowly until the base is firm and
   browned. Carefully turn the *ejjah* over to brown on top. The easiest
   way to do this is to turn it upside down on to a plate, then it can be
   slid back easily into the pan.

5 Serve cut into wedges with a salad such as Fattoush or Tabouleh
   (pages 38 and 36).

Variations on the basic ingredients
- Spinach, grated courgettes (zucchini) and onions.
- Minced (ground) meat with onions and mushrooms.
- Chives, parsley, mint, coriander (cilantro), spring onions (scallions) and
  potatoes.
- Walnuts, raisins and saffron with breadcrumbs.

EJJILITTAS
Tiny Herb Omelettes

S erve the omelittas hot or cold as a snack with a salad or a bowl of spiced chick peas (garbanzos). They should only be about 5 cm/2 in across.

◄§ S E R V E S 4 §►

4 eggs	1 bunch of parsley, finely chopped
½ bunch of chopped coriander (cilantro)	1 garlic clove, crushed
½ bunch of spring onions (scallions), finely chopped	30 ml / 2 tbsp oil

1 Beat the eggs well and stir in the remaining ingredients.

2 Heat the oil in a heavy frying pan (skillet). Drop in 15 ml/1 tbsp of the egg mixture at a time, filling the pan, but keeping each of the omelittas separate. When lightly cooked turn to brown on reverse side. Cook all the mixture this way.

3 May be served hot or cold.

HALAWIYEAT
SWEET PASTRIES AND DESSERTS

The most well known of all Arabic pastries must be *baklava* and *konafa*, a wonderful concoction of layered or shredded pastry and nuts steeped in a fragrant syrup. These pastries are made at home to celebrate religious days and festivals, weddings, birthdays and any special occasion. They are a delight to look at and a despair to the weight conscious!

The peoples of the Middle East and the Arabs in particular do seem to have a very sweet tooth. Hence the Egyptians produce that most marvellous of all sweet nuts the *marron glacé* – sweetened chestnuts – there is turkish delight from Turkey, and the countless number of sweetened nuts such as sugared almonds, the many-coloured sweet pumkin seeds and the *atari* syrup that is poured over pastries.

After a meal a variety of fruit may be offered and the essential strong black coffee.

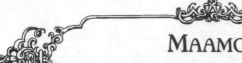

MAAMOUL
Date and Walnut Pastries

A wooden deeply carved mould called a tabi *is used to form these pastries into beautiful designs. The carvings are usually floral or geometric and may be bought in many different patterns.*

◆§ SERVES 4-6 §◆

FILLING	150 ml / ¼ pt / ⅔ cup water
225 g / 8 oz / 1⅓ cups stoned (pitted) dates, chopped	Icing (confectioners') sugar
5 ml / 1 tsp cinnamon	DOUGH
100 g / 4 oz / 1 cup almonds, chopped	450 g / 1 lb / 4 cups plain (all-purpose) flour
100 g / 4 oz / ½ cup sugar	225 g / 8 oz / 1 cup unsalted butter, melted
100 g / 4 oz / 1 cup walnuts, roughly chopped	30 ml / 2 tbsp rose water
	60-75 ml / 4-5 tbsp milk

1 Put the filling ingredients into a pan and cook over a low heat until the dates are soft and the water has been absorbed.

2 Make the dough: sift the flour, add the butter and mix by hand. Add the rose water and milk then knead the dough until it is soft and easy to mould.

3 Divide the dough into walnut sized pieces. Take one piece and roll it between your hands, then make a well in the centre, pinching up the sides.

4 Fill the hole with the date mixture then close and seal the top.

5 Slightly flatten each piece and place on a greased baking sheet. Continue until all the dough and filling have been used. If you have a *tabi* the filled dough can be gently pressed in, to take the design. If not make a pattern with a fork to help the icing sugar to adhere to the pastry.

6   Place the baking sheet in a pre-heated oven at 150°C/300°F/gas mark
    2 for about 30 minutes. Do not allow them to colour as they will
    become hard. Remove from the oven and when cool sprinkle with
    sifted icing sugar.

GHORAYEBAH
Almond Biscuits

*T*hese little biscuits or shortbread can be found in many different
    shapes and sizes all over the Middle East. They are easy to
make and delicious to eat; serve them with tea or coffee.

MAKES ABOUT 35 BISCUITS

450 g / 1 lb / 2 cups unsalted butter	450 g / 1 lb / 4 cups plain (all-purpose) flour, sifted
225 g / 8 oz / 1 cup icing (confectioners') sugar, sifted	About 35 blanched almonds

1   Beat the butter until pale and creamy; it will be easier to do if the
    butter is at room temperature.

2   Add the icing sugar a little at a time and continue to beat.

3   Add the flour, mixing well into the butter mixture.

4   Knead the dough by hand as it will now be quite firm. Continue to
    knead until it is smooth and pliable.

5   Take a small amount of dough in your hand (about the size of a
    walnut), roll into a sausage, then join the ends to make a circle.

6   Place an almond over the join and place on a greased baking sheet,
    leaving a little space between each one.

7   Bake in the oven at 150°C/300°F/gas mark 2 for about 20 minutes.
    The almonds should be a light golden brown, but the biscuit still
    white.

EL M'HANCHA
Almond Snake Cake

So called because the pastry is coiled round like a snake. This very popular cake is made from filo pastry with an almond paste rolled inside and the whole coiled into a spiral and baked.

◆§ SERVES 6 §◆

225 g / 8 oz / 2 cups ground almonds	30 g / 1 oz / 2 tbsp butter, melted
15 ml / 1 tbsp icing (confectioner's) sugar	6 sheets filo pastry
5 ml / 1 tsp cinnamon	Flour and water paste
90 ml / 6 tbsp orange flower or rose water	1 egg, beaten
	DECORATION
	Icing (confectioner's) sugar
	Cinnamon

1   Mix together the almonds, sugar, cinnamon, orange flower or rose water and the butter to make a thick paste. Knead, adding a little water if necessary to enable the paste to be rolled into long pencil shapes. They should be a little shorter than the filo pastry sheets.

2   Cover 5 sheets of filo pastry with a damp tea towel (dish cloth). Lay the sixth sheet on a work surface and place one almond stick along one edge. Roll the sheet up as tightly as possible and cover it with another damp tea towel.

3   Spread the next sheet out and place on another almond stick. Run a thin line of flour and water paste along the short edge, then overlap the first rolled up pastry on to the pasted edge. Now roll up the second length, so that the two are now joined together. Carefully roll up tightly into a spiral and place on a large greased flat tin. Cover with the damp towel.

4   Repeat with the next two sheets adding them on as before, taking care to overlap the joins so that they do not show. Repeat with the last two sheets. The spiral should be 25–30 cm/10-12 in in diameter.

5 Brush over the whole coil with beaten egg and bake in the oven at 190°C/375°F/gas mark 5 for 10 minutes until pale brown in colour. Turn the spiral over and return to the oven until it is golden brown.

6 Remove from the oven and turn over again. Sprinkle the whole surface with a thin layer of icing sugar. Place on to a serving plate and then very carefully draw thin lines of cinnamon over the white icing sugar.

KAAK SAGHIR BITTAMR
Little Date Cakes

T hese simple little cakes make a delightful dessert. They are not as sweet as some Arabic cakes, relying on the dates rather than added sugar.

◆§ SERVES 4-6 §◆

225 g / 8 oz / 1⅓ cups chopped stoned (pitted) dates	175 g / 6 oz / 1½ cups plain (all-purpose) flour
50 g / 2 oz / ½ cup chopped walnuts	Oil to shallow fry
50 g / 2 oz / ¼ cup melted butter	Double (heavy) cream

1 Place the dates in a large bowl then add the walnuts and butter and mix well.

2 Stir in the flour to form a stiff mixture.

3 Form the mixture into little cakes about 5 cm/2 in in diameter

4 Heat a little oil and fry (sauté) each cake until lightly browned on both sides. Serve with a spoonful of cream on each cake.

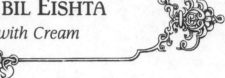

KONAFA BIL EISHTA
Konafa with Cream

*T*he *vermicelli-like pastry is filled with a ground rice cream, one could call it the Eastern equivalent to the French* Crème Patissière. *The pastry called* konafa *can be bought ready made from some delicatessens. It is almost impossible to make at home. Use either the cream or the nut filling.*

◄§ S E R V E S 4 – 6 §►

CREAM FILLING	NUT FILLING
60 ml / 4 tbsp ground rice	275 g / 10 oz / 1¼ cups pistachios, walnuts, almonds or hazelnuts or a mixture with 5 ml/1 tsp cinnamon (the nuts must be coarsely chopped)
60 ml / 4 tbsp cornflour (cornstarch)	
1.25 l / 2¼ pts / 5½ cups milk	
75 ml / 5 tbsp sugar	**SYRUP**
30 ml / 2 tbsp rose or orange flower water	450 g / 1 lb / 2 cups sugar
	300 ml / ½ pt / 1¼ cups water
225 g / 8 oz / 2 cups ground almonds	15 ml / 1 tbsp lemon juice
150 ml / ¼ pt / ⅔ cup double (heavy) cream	30 ml / 2 tbsp rose or orange flower water
450 g / 1 lb konafa pastry (paste)	**DECORATION**
225 g / 8 oz / 1 cup unsalted butter	75 g / 3 oz / ¾ cup finely chopped pistachios

1   To make the cream filling, mix the ground rice and cornflour to a paste with a little of the milk. Boil the remaining milk with the sugar. Pour a little of the hot milk into the paste, mix well and then pour back into the pan. Bring to a simmer, stirring all the time to prevent it becoming lumpy.

2   Cook for 1-2 minutes, stirring, but be careful as it will burn very easily. Remove from the heat and add the rose or orange flower water and the almonds. When cold beat in the cream.

3 To make the pastry, melt the butter and leave to cool slightly. Put the raw konafa into a large bowl and pour over the melted butter.

4 Coat all the strands with the butter using your hands to pull the strands apart so that they do not stick together.

5 Spread half of the pastry evenly over the base of a shallow baking tin (pan). Spread *either* the cream *or* the nut filling over then cover with the remaining pastry.

6 Lightly press on the pastry with your hands to ensure that it all holds together.

7 Bake in the oven at 180°C/350°F/gas mark 4 for 45 minutes, then turn up the oven to 230°C/450°F/gas mark 8 for 15 minutes to brown to a light golden colour.

8 Meanwhile, prepare the syrup. Boil the sugar, water and lemon juice for about 10 minutes, it should be thick enough to coat the back of a spoon. Add the rose or orange flower water and simmer for 1 minute longer.

9 Leave the syrup to cool, then chill it.

10 Cut round the edge of the pastry and turn out on to a plate. Pour the syrup all over and sprinkle with the pistachio nuts. Cut into serving sized portions.

ATAR
Syrup

*A*n *Arabic pastry without atar is like a day without sunshine!
The syrup is used to pour over pastries and cakes that require
a little extra sweetening and to satisfy the very sweet tooth of the
Arabs.*

450 g / 1 lb / 2 cups sugar	7.5-15 ml / ½-1 tbsp lemon juice
300 ml / ½ pt / 1¼ cups water	15-30 ml / 1-2 tbsp rose water

1   Dissolve the sugar in the water and lemon juice and simmer until it
is thick enough to coat the back of a spoon. When it is cool add the
rose water. This may be stored in a jar in a cool place for a long time.

TAMAR MASHI
Stuffed Dates

A small *bowl of stuffed dates is very welcome served with coffee
after a meal. The characteristically Arabic syrup served with
them makes them a treat for anyone with a sweet tooth.*

◆§ SERVES 6-8 §◆

175 g / 6 oz / 1½ cups ground almonds	60 ml / 4 tbsp rose water
75 g / 3 oz / ⅓ cup icing (confectioners') sugar	450 g / 1 lb / 2⅔ cups dates
	Atar syrup (above)

1   Mix the almonds and sugar with enough rose water to make a very
firm paste, and knead well.

2   Remove the stones from the dates by making a long slit down one side. Replace each stone with a slightly larger amount of almond mixture. Place the finished stuffed dates on to a serving plate.

3   Heat the atar syrup and pour all over.

AL BATHEETH
Date Sweetmeat

*T*his sweetmeat is generally served in small, open bowls with coffee. However, they would also make an unusual gift.

◄§ SERVES 4 - 6 §►

1 cardamom pod, crushed	225 g / 8 oz / 1⅓ cups chopped, stoned (pitted) dates
65 g / 2½ oz / 5 tbsp butter	2.5 ml / ½ tsp ground ginger
150 g / 5 oz / 1¼ cups wholemeal (graham) flour	Icing (confectioners') sugar

1   Fry (sauté) the cardamom pod in the butter for 2 minutes.

2   Heat the flour in a large dry heavy pan until lightly browned, stirring all the time.

3   Mix together all the ingredients except the icing sugar, and leave to cool.

4   Roll 15 ml/1tbsp of the mixture into a ball using the icing sugar to dust. Repeat until all the mixture is used. Chill.

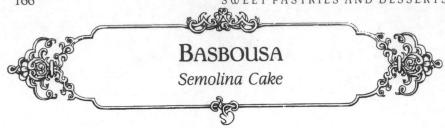

BASBOUSA
Semolina Cake

*T*his cake made with semolina has an interesting and unusual
texture and is most attractive to look at.

◄§ SERVES 4–6 §►

100 g / 4 oz / ½ cup butter	175 g / 6 oz / ¾ cup sugar
350 g / 12 oz / 2 cups semolina (cream of wheat)	2.5 ml / ½ tsp baking powder
175 g / 6 oz / 1½ cups self-raising (self rising) flour	120 ml / 4 fl oz / ½ cup natural (plain) yoghurt
175 g / 6 oz / 1½ cups desiccated (shredded) coconut	15 ml / 1 tbsp rose water
	75 g / 3 oz / ¾ cup halved almonds
	Atar syrup (page 164)

1   Melt the butter and add it to the semolina, flour, coconut, sugar and
    baking powder. Knead well.

2   Add the yoghurt, rose water and about 120 ml/4 fl oz/½ cup of warm
    water.

3   Pour into a square oiled baking dish (pan) and smooth over the
    surface.

4   Bake at 180°C/350°F/gas mark 4 for 30 minutes or until golden and
    firm to the touch. Cut the cake into diamond shapes and place an
    almond half in the centre of each diamond. Drench the hot cake with
    the cold Atar syrup.

ATAIF
Sweet Pancakes

*A*ll over the Arab Islamic world these pancakes make a symbolic appearance to mark the end of Ramadan – the month long fast. They are welcomed with joy and delight. They may be served hot or cold, sweet or with a savoury filling, with chopped nuts or clotted cream. I had this version from a friend in Bahrain.

SERVES 4 – 6

PANCAKES	FILLING
100 g / 4 oz / 1 cup plain (all-purpose) flour	225 g / 8 oz / 2 cups nuts of your choice, chopped
50 g / 2 oz / ¼ cup butter, melted	30 ml / 2 tbsp soft brown sugar
2 eggs, beaten	2.5 ml / ½ tsp nutmeg
300 ml / ½ pt / 1¼ cups milk, warmed	5 ml / 1 tsp ground cardamom
15 ml / 1 tbsp sugar	Atar syrup (page 164)
3-4 drops vanilla essence (extract)	DECORATION
	Ground pistachio nuts

1   Make the pancakes. Sift the flour in a bowl, add the butter, eggs, milk, sugar and vanilla essence. Mix well together and leave to stand for 15 minutes. The batter should be the consistency of single (light) cream.

2   Mix the filling ingredients together.

3   To make the pancakes, heat an omelette pan with a little oil and when very hot pour in enough batter to swirl around the pan. Arabic pancakes tend to be rather thicker than normal pancakes.

4   Cook the pancake until lightly brown then turn to cook the other side. Place it on a plate and put a spoonful of the filling in the centre, fold in half and keep warm. Continue with the remaining batter. When all are cooked, drench the pancakes with hot syrup and sprinkle with the ground pistachio nuts.

UM ALI
Ali's Mum's Pudding

*N*o collection of Arabic recipes would be complete without Ali's
Mum's Pudding. There are no records of from whence it
came, but Ali's Mum *must have been feeling in a creative mood as
this dessert is as popular with Arabs as it is with Westerners. It may
be made with puff or filo pastry (paste) or any left over bread.*

◄§ SERVES 4 - 6 §►

275-350 g / 10-12 oz puff pastry (paste) or 6 slices of bread, thinly sliced	1.2 l / 2 pts / 5 cups milk
	75-100 g / 3-4 oz sugar
100 g / 4 oz / ⅔ cup mixed dried fruit (fruit cake mix)	5 cloves
	5 ml / 1 tsp ground cardamom
175 g / 6 oz / 1½ cups mixed nuts, chopped	5 ml / 1 tsp cinnamon

1   Traditionally the filo or puff pastry was fried, but today we are more
     conscious of the food we eat and the way in which it is cooked, so I
     bake the pastry in the oven until it is crisp and lightly brown. If
     using bread, bake in the oven until lightly crisp. Break into small
     pieces and layer in a baking dish (pan) with the dried fruits, the nuts
     and the whole cloves.

2   Heat the milk with the sugar until it has all dissolved, then pour
     over the pastry.

3   Sprinkle over the spices and bake in the oven at 200°C/400°F/gas
     mark 8 for 20 minutes. The top should be lightly brown. Serve very
     hot.

AL ORZ POUDING

Rice Pudding

*T*his simple pudding is delicious just as it is. However, you can
include chopped walnuts or toasted almonds in the recipe for
extra flavour and texture.

◄§ SERVES 4 §►

900 ml / 1½ pt / 3¾ cups milk

300 ml / ½ pt / 1¼ cups water

100 g / 4 oz / ½ cup sugar

100 g / 4 oz / ½ cup pudding or
risotto rice

15 ml / 1 tbsp rose or orange
flower water

Pinch of cinnamon

1   Put the milk, water and sugar in a heavy pan, bring to the boil and
add the rice, stirring once.

2   Cover and simmer gently for 25 minutes.

3   Add the rose or orange flower water and continue to simmer for
another 5 minutes or until the rice is cooked.

4   Pour into serving bowls and leave to chill.

5   Just before serving sprinkle on the cinnamon.

MUHALLABEYA
Rice Pudding with Honey Sauce

*T*his is a variation on the usual recipe as it has a honey sauce.
Another variation is baked in the oven instead of on the top of
the stove.

◄§ SERVES 4-6 §►

1.2 l / 2 pts / 5 cups milk

100 g / 4 oz / ½ cup ground rice

75 g / 3 oz / ⅓ cup sugar

30-45 ml / 2-3 tbsp orange flower
or rose water

45 ml / 3 tbsp clear honey

75 g / 3 oz / ¾ cup mixed almonds
and pistachios, coarsely chopped

1   Bring the milk to the boil then mix the ground rice to a paste with
150 ml/¼ pt/⅔ cup water and pour into the milk, stirring vigorously.

2   Bring back to the boil very slowly, stirring all the time to prevent
lumps forming. Cook until the mixture thickens then add the sugar.

3   Add the orange flower or rose water and stir well. Pour into a
serving dish and leave to cool.

4   To make the syrup, mix the honey with 60-75 ml/4-5 tbsp of water,
warm up slowly so that the honey melts. Cool before pouring over
the dessert then decorate with the nuts.

AL ORZ AL HOKU
Sweet Rice

*T*his rice dish can be used as a dessert or it can also be served
with grilled lamb or chicken; it is eaten either hot or cold.
The cardamom pods and the saffron impart to this dish its special
flavour.

◄§ SERVES 4–6 §►

3 cardamom pods, cracked	450 g / 1 lb / 2 cups basmati rice, well washed
1.5 ml / ¼ tsp saffron threads	
30 ml / 2 tbsp rose water	Pinch of salt
1.5 l / 2½ pts / 6 cups water	100 g / 4 oz / ½ cup sugar or honey

50 g / 2 oz / ¼ cup butter

1   Place the cardamom pods and saffron into the rose water, set aside
    to steep.

2   Bring the water to boiling point then add the rice and salt. Stir
    occasionally until it returns to the boil.

3   Boil uncovered for 8 minutes, then drain into a sieve (strainer).

4   Put the rice into a large bowl then pour on the honey or sugar and
    mix thoroughly and lightly with a fork.

5   Heat the butter in a large pan then add the rice.

6   Sprinkle the rose water mixture over the top of the rice.

7   Cover the pan with a cloth or kitchen paper and a well fitting lid to
    keep the steam in and continue to cook slowly for about 20 minutes
    until cooked.

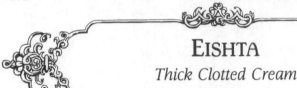
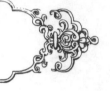

EISHTA
Thick Clotted Cream

*T*his is a delicious thick cream traditionally made by slowly cooking buffalo milk. A good substitute, however, can be made using cream and fresh cow's milk.

◄§ SERVES 4-6 §►

300 ml / ½ pt / 1¼ cups double (heavy) cream	900 ml / 1½ pts / 3¾ cups milk

1 Pour the cream and milk into a wide, shallow pan to give the greatest possible surface.

2 Bring slowly to the boil, and simmer gently over a very low heat for 1½ hours. Leave to stand for 6 hours or overnight, then chill.

3 A thick crust will form, which should be removed with a sharp knife or a slotted spoon.

4 Serve with pastries, pancakes and desserts.

LOOSE HILOO
Sweet Almonds

*W*hole shelled nuts that are fried in butter and dusted in sugar may be eaten at the end of a meal or as a snack. They would also make delightful presents.

◄§ SERVES 4-6 §►

225 g / 8 oz / 1 cup almonds	50 g / 2 oz / ¼ cup butter
Icing (confectioners') sugar	

1 Stir-fry the nuts in the butter for 2-3 minutes.

2 Remove from the pan, cool and then dust lightly with icing sugar.

3 These may be stored in a tin and will keep fresh for a month or so.

SIMSIMIYA
Sesame Seed Brittle

S erve this as a sweet to finish a meal or simply as a treat.

◄§ SERVES 4 - 6 §►

150 g / 5 oz / scant ½ cup honey	1 kg / 2 lb / 4 cups roasted sesame seeds
350 g / 12 oz / 1½ cups sugar	

1 Simmer the honey and sugar until it reaches the hard ball stage, stirring continuously. Test by dropping a spoonful into cold water. It should form a small hard ball.

2 Add the sesame seeds and mix thoroughly together.

3 Spread on to a warm, oiled baking sheet.

4 Cut into diamonds and leave to cool.

TAMAR
Dates

*D*ates have always played an important part in the culinary life
of the Arab world. There are over 300 varieties ranging in
colour from pale gold to red to dark brown. They can be seen in
the vegetable souk piled in great slabs.

Dates have been growing in the Middle East for many
centuries. When out in the desert one can come unexpectedly upon
an oasis where the date palms flourish.

When they are eaten fresh from the tree they are crisp and
juicy, though not as sweet as when they have been stored for some
time. They may be frozen without any deterioration.

Dates, which are eaten all the year round, are used extensively
in cooking. They are one of the first foods to be eaten during the
holy month of Ramadan, when Muslims do not eat or drink from
sunrise to sunset. Then the cannon is fired to announce that the sun
has set and the call to prayer can be heard coming from the tall,
stately minarets. It will shortly be time to eat.

The date palm was used in its entirety. When no longer
producing dates, the trunk would be used for building purposes and
the great branches were cut and used for the walls of dwelling
places known as Barasti houses. This was an excellent method of
building walls, as the leaves were not at all dense so the wind
could go straight through the room, thereby giving a little coolness.
Barasti houses can still be seen today in some of the desert areas.

AL FAWAKIH
Fruit

*F*ruit can be seen in the souks in great abundance and variety:
huge dark green watermelons or the small oval bright
honeydew variety, mangoes, dark purple figs, red plums, apricots
and bananas of all sizes, from the tiniest to the large plantains that
are used for cooking. Fruit is bought by the box and is eaten at any
time, usually fresh.

The Arabs do make lovely compotes of fresh or dried fruit with nuts. These too are eaten frequently, as well as being added to almost any cooked food.

There are apricots that have been dried and pressed into large thin sheets called amardine. *This is used for desserts or drinks, though the children will, if no one is looking, take a piece or two, roll it into a ball and pop it into their mouths – delicious.*

Amardine makes a delicious puréed dessert. Soak about 6 sheets in plenty of water for a few hours, then simmer gently until it is reduced to a pulp, add sugar to taste and continue to simmer until you have a rich purée. To serve put the purée into a bowl, sprinkle over a few toasted almonds and chill. Alternatively, use dried apricots soaked overnight or the ready-to-eat variety.

A variation on the above would be to add cream whipped in with the purée or it may be served separately.

KHOSHAF
Dried Fruit Salad

T his fruit salad uses only dried fruit and nuts. It is an Arabic favourite that can be made with any combination of fruit, but to be classically correct only apricots, raisins and nuts should be used.

❧ SERVES 4-6 ❧

450 g / 1 lb / 2⅔ cups dried apricots	50 g / 2 oz / ½ cup toasted almond halves
225 g / 8 oz / 1⅓ cups raisins	50 g / 2 oz / ½ cup pistachio nuts
100 g / 4 oz / 1 cup blanched almonds	30 ml / 2 tbsp rose or orange flower water

1 Wash the fruits if necessary, put them into a large bowl with the nuts, cover with warm water and sugar to taste. Do not add too much sugar as it will spoil the flavour of the fruit.

2 Add the rose or orange flower water and leave to soak for 2 days, by which time the fruits will have swelled and the juice will be rich and thick.

COUSCOUS BI SUKKAR
Sweet Couscous

This is the sweet version of the savoury couscous and is delicious. The couscous is served in a pyramid shape with sugar and cinnamon poured down the sides in streams.

SERVES 4-6

60 ml / 4 tbsp raisins	**DECORATION**
450 g / 1 lb / 2⅔ cups couscous	Icing (confectioners') sugar
100 g / 4 oz / ½ cup butter, melted	Cinnamon

1 Soak the raisins until they swell; orange juice adds a lovely flavour.

2 Sprinkle a little water over the grains of couscous, using your hands to prevent any lumps from forming.

3 Place the couscous in a sieve (strainer) or steamer and steam for 30 minutes or according to the directions on the packet.

4 Sprinkle with the melted butter, and fork over from time to time.

5 When cooked, place on a serving plate and make into a pyramid. Mix the icing sugar with some cinnamon and the raisins and dribble down the sides. Serve warm.

KHOOBOUS
BREAD AND PASTRIES

'His bread is kneaded and his water jug is full.' This is an Arabic saying that refers to a man who has everything. There is an abundance of sayings in the Arab world that express the importance of bread in the lives of us all.

In the Middle East, which encompasses many different countries, bread is as varied in the names and the spelling as in the shapes in which it is made. *Khoubiz* or *khobz* or *pitta* bread is the standard flat leavened bread. *Manaiysh*, a Lebanese spicy bread, has a mixture of olive oil and *zaatar* spread over the surface before baking. *Khoubiz basali* is a Syrian onion bread. *Saluf bi hilbeh* is a Yemeni spicy bread; and there are many others. The shapes vary through large, small, round, oval and rectangular. However, the basic recipe is more or less the same, using a strong (bread) brown or white flour with yeast as the raising agent.

An Arabic meal would not be complete without plenty of *khoubiz*. To many people, it replaces the knife and fork. Using their right hand only, they break off small pieces of bread, fold it in half to form a 'spoon', and use this to scoop up the food.

Kaak is another form of bread, but unlike the *khoubiz* the *kaaks* are well cooked until they are crisp and hard all through, very similar to a rusk. This also uses the basic dough ingredients but with the addition of various flavourings such as

177

mahlab which is the kernel from the stones of black cherries which are dried and ground to a powder. The *Kaahk Ramazan*, traditionally only baked during the holy month of Ramadan, when all good Muslims do not allow a drop of water, or a morsel of food, to touch their lips from sunrise to sunset. So toward evening the fragrance of freshly baked *kaak* pours out of homes and bakeries inviting everyone to break their fast with these delicious little rusks, served with a milk or fruit drink and dates.

KHUBIZ
Basic Dough

*T*his basic recipe can be used in all kinds of ways and served at any Arab-style meal. It is a simple, flat bread made from a plain leavened dough.

⋅⧫ SERVES 4 – 6 ⧫⋅

14 g / ½ oz / 1 tsp fresh yeast

or 7 g / ¼ oz / ½ tsp dried yeast

2.5 ml / ½ tsp sugar

300 ml / ½ pt / 1¼ cups warm water

450 g / 1 lb / 4 cups strong (bread) flour

2.5 ml / ½ tsp salt

1   Put the yeast into a small bowl with 45-60 ml/3-4 tbsp of the warm water, stir in the sugar and leave to stand in a warm place for 15 minutes or until it becomes frothy. If using dried yeast, follow the directions on the packet.

2   Sift the flour and salt into a warmed mixing bowl.

3   When the yeast is active make a well in the centre of the flour and pour in the yeast mixture, add enough warm water to make a firm but not hard dough.

4   Lightly flour a surface then knead the dough vigorously with your hands for about 15 minutes until it is smooth and pliable.

5   If you like a softer bread, add 15 ml/1 tbsp of oil and knead well into the dough.

6 With oiled hands form the dough into a ball. The oil will prevent the dough from cracking or forming a crust as it rises.

7 Cover the bowl with a damp cloth and leave in a warm place to rise for about 2 hours. It should double in bulk.

8 Knock back the dough and knead for a few minutes.

9 Divide the mixture into 6 or more pieces, depending on the size you want.

10 Lightly flour a surface, then flatten out each piece with a rolling pin or your hands until they are about 5 mm/¼ in thick, keeping them as circular as possible. Dust with a little flour and cover with a cloth. Leave to rise for 20-30 minutes.

11 Heat the oven to very hot, 230°C/450°F/gas mark 8. When the oven has reached temperature heat two greased baking sheets, being careful not to let them burn.

12 When all is ready, remove the sheets from the oven and carefully slide the dough rounds on to the hot sheets, sprinkle a few drops of water on to the dough to prevent them from browning, and bake for 10 minutes.

13 Do not open the oven door during this time, but after 10 minutes look to make sure the dough has puffed up. Remove from the baking sheets and immediately put on to wire racks to cool. They should be soft and white with a pocket inside.

Variations:

- **Thyme and sesame seed** *(Manaaish Bil Zaatar)*
  Brush the tops with a little olive oil and sprinkle with zaatar (page 13), sesame seeds or chopped walnuts prior to baking.

- A lovely snack is to make a depression in the dough, break an egg into it before it goes into the oven, and sprinkle with salt and pepper. The egg will set as the bread is cooked.

- Another savoury is fried (sautéed) minced (ground) lamb which can be mixed into the dough with various herbs before it is cooked.

- Mix 100 g/4 oz/1 cup sesame seeds and 100 g/4 oz/½ cup sugar to a paste with a little oil. Spread on top of the dough before baking. It will give a delightfully sweet 'cake'.

180
BREAD AND PASTRIES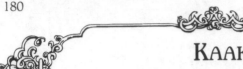

KAAK
Rusks with Sesame Seeds

E arly one chilly winter morning, sitting wrapped in a blanket
near to the window, watching the early morning hustle and
bustle of the village, my host brought in a dish of newly baked hard
rusks covered in sesame seeds. She showed how the kaaks were
dunked into steaming mugs of hot sweetened milk before being
devoured by the hungry.

The kaaks are baked in many shapes and sizes from 5 cm/2 in
squares to 15 cm/6 in long rolls. The particular flavouring is
mahlab, the pip inside the kernel of the black cherry. The pips are
always sold whole to be ground into a powder when needed.

◄§ SERVES 4 – 6 §►

50 g / 2 oz / 4 tsp fresh yeast or 25 g / 1 oz / 2 tsp dried yeast	5 ml / 1 tsp salt
Lukewarm water	2.5 ml / ½ tsp mahlab (or a few drops of almond essence [extract])
2.5 ml / ½ tsp sugar	225 g / 8 oz / 1 cup butter, melted
1 kg / 2 lb / 8 cups plain (all-purpose) flour, sifted	1 egg, beaten
	Sesame seeds

1 Put the yeast into a small bowl with 45-60 ml/3-4 tbsp of lukewarm
water. Add the sugar and leave to stand in a warm place for 15
minutes or until the froth appears. If using dried yeast, follow the
directions on the packet.

2 Mix the flour, salt and mahlab together.

3 Pour the yeast and butter into the flour adding enough warm water
to form a soft but not sticky dough. Vigorously knead the dough for
15 minutes until soft and pliable.

4 With oiled hands form the dough into a ball. Place in a bowl and
cover with a damp cloth. Set aside in a warm place to rise. It should
double in size, taking about 2 hours.

5   Knock back the dough, kneading for a few minutes. Make into rolls, squares or a shape of your choice. Brush each piece with a little beaten egg, sprinkle on the sesame seeds and place on to oiled baking sheets. Leave to rise again for 30 minutes.

6   Bake at 180°C/350°F/gas mark 4 for 20 minutes. Lower the heat to 150°C/300°F/gas mark 2 for a further 1 hour or until the kaak has completely dried out to a golden colour. These may be stored for many weeks in an airtight container.

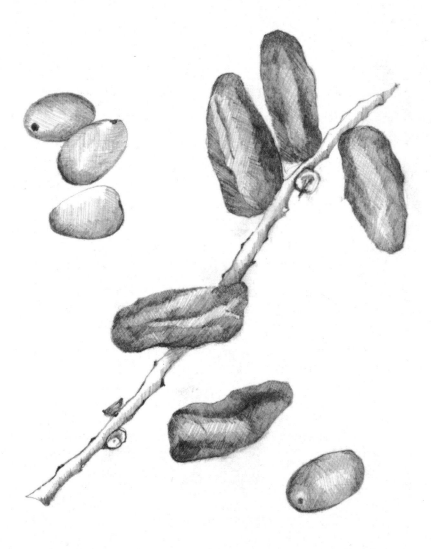

LAHM BI AJEEN
Lamb Pies

*T*hese are little flat lamb pies made with khoubiz dough. They
are so popular that they are to be found in bakeries all over
the Middle East and are eaten as an occasional snack or as part of
the mezza.

◄§ SERVES 4 – 6 §►

30 ml / 2 tbsp oil	1.5 ml / ¼ tsp cinnamon
1 large onion, finely chopped	Salt and pepper
450 g / 1 lb / 2 cups minced (ground) lamb	2 tomatoes, chopped
100 g / 4 oz / 1 cup pine nuts	15 ml / 1 tbsp grenadine or lemon juice
1.5 ml / ¼ tsp allspice	One quantity of khoubiz dough (page 178)

1   Heat the oil in a large pan and fry (sauté) the onion until soft, add
the lamb and continue to fry until it changes colour and is crumbly.

2   Add the pine nuts, spices, salt and pepper to taste, stir fry for a few
minutes then add the tomatoes. Cover and cook on a low heat for 10
minutes.

3   Stir in the grenadine or lemon juice and leave to cool. The mixture
should be moist but not liquid.

4   Punch down the dough after its initial rising.

5   Take off a piece of dough about the size of an egg and roll or press
into a round about 10 cm/4 in in diameter. Repeat until all the
dough is used.

6   Place the rounds on an oiled baking sheet and flute up the sides
with the fingertips.

7   Spread 15 ml/1 tbsp of filling on to each round and leave to rest for
10 minutes. Sprinkle the edges of the dough with a little water to
prevent the dough from browning.

8 Bake in a hot oven at 220°C/425°F/gas mark 8 for 8-10 minutes. The pastries should be well done but not brown as they should be soft enough to roll up and eat with the fingers.

Variations

- A shortcrust pastry (basic pie crust) can be used instead of the *khoubiz*.

- *Khoubiz Addas:* this is an Iraqi favourite that is said to relieve acute anxiety. The filling is mixed in with the dough, rather than placed on top.

AJAIN DOU MADAKIN MOUSHAHIN
Savoury Pastries

*S*avoury pastries like their sweet counterparts are very popular in the Middle East; they will appear at any time and of any flavour. To go into a bakery shop and see row upon row of these delicious savouries is a mouthwatering experience, and woe betide those on a diet.

The making of filo pastry is an art that takes many years to master. A tennis ball size of dough is stretched and rolled until it reaches 4 ft (1.2 m) in diameter, by which time it is almost transparent. However, the commercially made filo is quite acceptable. I have also used puff pastry to replace the filo when that was unobtainable.

The filling and the shapes that encompass each type of filling are open to almost any combination, but I have given a chart of shapes with their usual fillings below. To cook the pastries, they are traditionally fried in deep oil, but they could as easily be baked in a hot oven if preferred.

Pastry	Filling	Shape
Filo	Spinach	Triangular
Filo	Cheese and mint	Cigar
Unleavened bread	Minced (ground) meat	Disc
Puff pastry	Chicken	Any
Any bread	Zaatar	Disc
Any	Cheese	Any
Filo	Peas and potatoes	Triangular

FILLINGS

Al Khodar
Spinach

450 g / 1 lb fresh spinach	30 ml / 2 tbsp chopped parsley
1 onion, finely chopped	30 ml / 2 tbsp pine nuts
15 ml / 1 tbsp olive oil	Salt and pepper

1 Wash the spinach in plenty of water, then put into a pan and cook for 4-5 minutes.

2 Squeeze the moisture out then chop finely.

3 Fry (sauté) the onions in the oil until soft, add the remaining ingredients and check the seasoning.

4 Prepare the pastry of your choice to use with the filling.

5 If using filo dough it is crispier if deep fried.

Burek Sigara
Cheese and Mint

1 egg, beaten	15 ml / 1 tbsp chopped mint
225 g / 8 oz / 1 cup soft cheese	

1 Add the beaten egg and the mint to the cheese, mixing well together.

2 Prepare the pastry of your choice, fill and shape.

3 These may be deep fried or baked in a hot oven.

Minced Meat

1 large onion, chopped	5 ml / 1 tsp baharat (page 14)
15 ml / 1 tbsp oil	15 ml / 1 tbsp lemon juice
450 g / 1 lb / 2 cups minced (ground) lamb or beef	30 ml / 2 tbsp pine nuts
	Salt and pepper

1 Fry the onion in the oil until it is brown, then add the meat. Continue to fry, adding the remaining ingredients.

2 Do not let the mixture dry out, adding a little water if necessary. It should be moist, but not wet.

3 Use as required.

Variations

• Tomato juice may replace the water

• Cumin, coriander (cilantro) or other spices may be used instead of baharat.

Chicken

Left over cooked chicken may be chopped and added to a little white sauce made from chicken stock. Use as in the previous fillings.

Zaatar
Herb

This is a dried herb mixture of sesame seeds and a variety of a Middle Eastern thyme.

Spoon a little oil on to an uncooked piece of *khubiz* dough and then sprinkle the zaatar over the top. Bake in a hot oven. This is also very good if 5 ml/1 tsp of zaatar is mixed with a little olive oil and spread over a piece of bread. Place under a grill (broiler) for a minute or two.

Cheese

Small cubes of Feta or Haloumi cheese may be wrapped in triangles of filo pastry and fried rapidly in hot oil.

Peas and Potato

Cooked potato diced and mixed with fried onions, baharat (page 14) and peas, put into a pastry of your choice and fried or baked.

FAWAKH
DRINKS

After the evening meal when the bright stars are out, groups of Arabs may be seen, with their shoes to one side, sitting cross-legged on a carpet on the pavements or outside their houses, drinking coffee and perhaps smoking the hubble-bubble pipe. Card playing or backgammon is a popular pastime of an evening, and pots of incense may be burned or handed round from person to person to waft under their cloths. Sweet pastries are occasionally served at this time.

Coffee drinking plays an important part in Arabic culture. Whether it is a business partner, friend or a passing stranger, all are offered coffee or tea. The cups will be tiny, usually without handles. In the past they would be made of brass but today they are usually china or glass, decorated with Arabic symbols or words from the *Koran*.

Rules of etiquette must be observed in the serving of coffee. The person of highest rank will be served first, followed by the eldest and so on down to the youngest person. Two or three cups are expected to be drunk. When a guest has finished, the cup is shaken from side to side or turned upside-down. As the sugar is part of the making process guests are always asked how their coffee is preferred, sweet, medium or unsweetened. Coffee may be made in a *kanaka*, a small long handled pot, or in a *dullah*. These are of many sizes, very elegant and occasionally with an intricate design beaten into the brass. The spouts are long and curved. The lid has a high decoratively shaped spire on top that is hollow. It has been said the hollow area was for putting coffee beans in. The rattling noise the beans would make if someone were to try and steal the pot of coffee or to put poison in the coffee would be a warning!

The coffee beans are ground to a fine powder, and occasionally ground cardamoms or cinnamon may be added.

QUAHWAH
Coffee

*T*o make a strong brew, add 150 ml/5 fl oz/¾ cup water to 10 ml/2 tsp ground beans. Add 10 ml/1 heaped tsp of sugar to sweeten.

1   Boil the water in the pot, then add the coffee and sugar. Return to the heat and bring back to the boil. When the froth rises remove from the heat and stir.

2   Repeat the process once again, then leave to stand until the grounds have settled. Serve in small cups.

LABAN
Yoghurt Drink

*L*aban is one of the most popular of drinks. It may be bought in many flavours but is easily made at home. Simply stir a few tablespoonfuls of yoghurt into a glass of milk or water. Sugar or salt may be added. Adding a spoonful of finely chopped mint leaves makes a very refreshing drink. It is always served chilled, sometimes with crushed ice or carbonated water.

SHAI WA MASHROUB FAWAKH
Tea and Fruit Drinks

*T*ea is also a popular drink, usually served in tiny glass cups set
into metal holders, often on a matching tray. A variety of spices
may be added, as in the refreshing Moroccan mint tea. Lemon is
also used with saffron and cinnamon added with the tea leaves.

Perhaps because of the Moslem prohibition of alcohol, Arabs
have a passion for fruit drinks which they have perfected to a fine
art. In the small street bars, fruits of many varieties are piled high
in glass fronted cases. Intricate blends of fruit and sweet cream or
milk and sugar are poured in swirls, into tall handled glasses and
topped with ground pistachio or whole pine nuts. Almost any fresh
fruit is used, including lemons, watermelon, passion fruit and
pomegranates. Like a scene from the past, street juice vendors still
beckon the thirsty with gigantic glass jars of drinks such as the dark
purple jallab, rose pink or green, mint-flavoured water, brown
tamarind and an almost black liquorice. Almonds, orange flower
water and cornflour (cornstarch) are a traditional milky blend.

Prior to the advent of refrigeration, fresh fruit was dried or
made into thick syrups or pastes with sugar to be added to cool
water later.

These juices will keep for about two weeks. To use, add cold
water to taste.

Orange: The juice is boiled with sugar to produce a thick syrup.

Mulberry: A little orange juice may be added to this, then it is boiled
with sugar.

Apricots: These are usually dried and reduced to a pulp – *amardine*. It
will need soaking for several hours.

Tamarind: Clean and wash the tamarind thoroughly before soaking
overnight in water. Sieve (strain) to a purée before adding sugar, bring to
the boil and simmer until a thick syrup forms.

Liquorice: The root is steeped as in tea making or it may be turned into
a syrup with sugar.

Pomegranates: The pulp and juice are extracted and the juice boiled with
sugar to a syrup.

ATER HELOW
Sweet Fragrances

*D*uring the 10th century an Arabian doctor and philosopher
called Avicenna discovered how to extract the aromatic
properties of flowers. The original formula, using the highly scented
Cabbage Rose, can be found in his book on chemistry. Since then,
the use of rose water for cooking or washing the hands of special
guests has gained in popularity in the Arab world.

The mystique of frankincense and myrrh goes back to biblical
times, but it is still in every day use by the Arabs. The process that
Marco Polo described more than 700 years ago is still in practice.
The resin is taken from frankincense trees that once grew in the
southern Gulf but are now only found in Dhofar and northern
Somalia. On occasions the strong fragrant pieces of incense, called
oud, are burned in containers of pottery or metal-lined wood, the
spirals of smoke come drifting out through the holes like an
Aladdin's lamp. These are passed round from person to person to be
wafted under their clothes or in their faces. There might also be
fragrant oils, another Arab speciality for special occasions.

INDEX